HITLER'S WAR MACHINE

THE OFFICIAL U-BOAT COMMANDER'S HANDBOOK
The Illustrated Edition

EDITED BY BOB CARRUTHERS

Pen & Sword
MARITIME

This edition published in 2013 by
Pen & Sword Maritime
An imprint of
Pen & Sword Books Ltd
47 Church Street
Barnsley
South Yorkshire
S70 2AS

First published in Great Britain in 2011 in digital format by
Coda Books Ltd.

ISBN 978 1 78159 158 1

The right of Bob Carruthers to be identified as Author of this work has been asserted
by him in accordance with the Copyright, Designs and Patents Act 1988.

A CIP catalogue record for this book is
available from the British Library

Printed and bound by
CPI Group (UK) Ltd, Croydon, CR0 4YY

Pen & Sword Books Ltd incorporates the Imprints of Pen & Sword Aviation, Pen &
Sword Family History, Pen & Sword Maritime, Pen & Sword Military, Pen & Sword
Discovery, Pen & Sword Politics, Pen & Sword Atlas, Pen & Sword Archaeology,
Wharncliffe Local History, Wharncliffe True Crime, Wharncliffe Transport, Pen &
Sword Select, Pen & Sword Military Classics, Leo Cooper, The Praetorian Press,
Claymore Press, Remember When, Seaforth Publishing and Frontline Publishing

For a complete list of Pen & Sword titles please contact
PEN & SWORD BOOKS LIMITED
47 Church Street, Barnsley, South Yorkshire, S70 2AS, England
E-mail: enquiries@pen-and-sword.co.uk
Website: www.pen-and-sword.co.uk

CONTENTS

INTRODUCTION

For the brave men who manned the U-boat fleet the uneven struggle played out between 1939 and 1945 was a real tragedy of catastrophic proportions. In 1939 at the very outset of the war it was already clear to Karl Dönitz that the U-boat mission was futile. As weapon systems, the Type II and Type VII U-boats of 1939 were already inadequate for the task ahead and there were simply not enough of them. To make matters worse, their torpedoes were faulty and their enemies were infinitely superior in every material respect. In their capacity for raw courage and endurance the men of the U-boat fleet demonstrated their determination and dedication to duty.

However, despite some justifiable anxiety, the men of the British Royal Navy and their allies were never close to being outmatched by the U-boats and proved themselves equally tough, resolute and, when occasion demanded, they too would prove totally ruthless.

In December 1941 when Hitler made his typically misguided decision to declare war on the USA the balance tipped even further away from the U-boat fleet. The immense resources of the US Navy and air force secured the prospect of victory. As new aircraft types came into service and Iceland was opened up to allied aircraft the "air gap", the unprotected patch of the mid Atlantic, grew ever smaller. In 1944 the air gap was closed altogether but by then Dönitz had finally accepted defeat in the North Atlantic and ordered his U-boats to withdraw.

A willingness to make the supreme sacrifice in the face of insurmountable odds can be viewed as a noble quality, but it is still futile nonetheless. Blood will never overcome steel and the slender resources of the U-boat fleet were insufficient to bring about the strategic victory which they strived to produce.

Despite all of the odds ranged against them, the U-boats did, for a brief time, succeed in wreaking tremendous havoc among allied shipping, and during its short ascendancy the U-boat fleet gave Churchill one of his most genuine and serious bouts of concern for Britain's continued survival. So serious were Churchill's concerns that he later confessed that the Battle of the Atlantic was "the only thing that ever frightened me."

The U-Boat flotillas are in their bases. The boats are waiting to go on a long-range mission. They are England's most sinister opponents.

The obvious dangers of serving in the U-boat fleet combined with the highly persuasive activities of the Nazi propaganda machine put a strong gloss on the U-boat war which lionised the achievements of men like Gunter Prein, Joachim Schepke and Otto Kretschmer, but it was a telling statistic that by 1941 two of these heroes were dead and the third was in allied captivity.

It is notoriously difficult to measure the effectiveness of the U-boat campaign. There is no question that the U-boat activities proved massively destructive. Obviously a great deal of vital war equipment and supplies were denied to the allies, but the allied ship yards, particularly after America entered the war proved themselves capable of replenishing the losses and eventually

Mountains of provisions, almost all in tins (e.g., the "tin oxes") are piled on the wharf and on the walkways. Even the bo'sun, the "Number I" for the first watch officer, responsible for everything to do with the sailors on board, helps out. There is so much that has to be sent out with the boat on its long-range mission.

the tonnage launched far outstripped the rate of loss, and despite all of the endeavours to the contrary the allied mercantile fleets actually grew in size as the war progressed.

There was clearly a massive material loss and a damaging effect on allied morale the reverberations of which, as we have seen, reached as far as Churchill himself. However, the actual statistics are difficult to assess with certainty and it is impossible to come up with an overall measure of success or failure's - boats were involved in mine laying exercises as well as direct attacks on allied ships. What is known is that altogether nine U-boats were lost in the first five months of war in 1939 and the sinking of 122 merchant ships was directly attributed to U-boat action. In 1939, the first calendar year of the war, for every U-boat lost, some thirteen allied ships were being sent to the bottom.

Twenty-four U-boats were lost during 1940 against a loss of 471 allied ships, the loss of which were attributed to U-boat action. This was to prove to be the high point of the U-boats with almost twenty allied ships sunk in exchange for each U-boat which was lost.

In 1941, the turning point of the war in the Atlantic was already in sight. The rate of U-boat losses continued to climb with 35 boats sunk for a reduced annual tally of 432 ships sunk by U-boat action. An exchange rate of just over twelve allied ships sunk for each U-boat sunk. A lower rate than had been achieved in the first year of the war and a sharp decline on 1940.

During 1942, the rate of U-boat destruction rose sharply as 86 boats were sunk in return for 1159 allied ships. This was approaching the level of destruction which, if maintained, could actually threaten the lifeline to the UK and it was this dark hour which gave Churchill serious grounds for concern. Despite all the extra resources deployed by The Kriegsmarine however, the rate of ships sunk by each boat lost steadfastly hovered around thirteen.

By 1943, the Enigma breakthrough was having its effect. Convoy tactics had improved, air cover and radar had improved dramatically and in consequence the number of U-boats sunk climbed to a catastrophic 242 boats. Only 463 allied ships had been sunk in return. The exchange rate had fallen from thirteen allied ships sunk for every U-boat lost in 1942 to just under two allied ships sunk for each U-boat lost in 1943. The allies could make good their losses but with the fortunes of war running against Germany on every front, the evidence was now plain to see - the U-boat cause was hopeless. The rapidly mounting losses and other important factors such as the constantly shifting balance of technology in favour of the allies, who were gaining in firepower, resources and tonnage of shipping launched, all conspired to render the decision to carry on the battle beyond 1943 criminally suicidal.

With the Enigma code now cracked and the allies in receipt of detailed operational information the consequences were likely to be calamitous. Dönitz remained blissfully unaware of the Enigma developments but it was clear that the battle for the Atlantic convoy routes had been lost and Dönitz ordered his boats to withdraw from the North Atlantic. Elsewhere he was forced to continue the uneven fight. The result was disastrous for the brave men of The Kriegsmarine. 250 U-boats were sunk in 1944, which unsurprisingly was the worst year of the war so far for U-boat losses. In return for this alarming rate of loss, the Grey Wolves sank just 132 ships which meant that almost two U-boats were now being lost for each allied ship sunk.

The advent of airborne radar and advanced submarine detection devices should have signalled the end of the fight. By 1944, the U-boat war had clearly been lost and despite the desperate search for effective counter measures and improved U-boat designs there was simply no way back. Still there was to be no respite for the U-boats. 1945 was even worse with

120 boats destroyed in action for the loss of just 56 allied ships during the first few months of the year before the final peace arrived early in May 1945. By the end of the war over two U-boats were being sunk for each allied ship which was sent to the bottom.

All together 731 U-boats were lost in combat between 1939 and 1945. A further 200 were scuttled as part of Operation Regenbogen in May 1945. This massive sacrifice of men and resources represented the equivalent resource needed to field

More than 40 men on a boat want to be looked after for months to come. The last thing to roll onto the wharf, on the day of the trip if possible, is the fresh produce: lemons, potatoes, vegetables, meat, for the first 8 days. It won't keep any longer on board. Apples are only good for 14 days. The fresh bread will then be ringed with heavy mould and be rotten inside. It's then known as "rabbit" because of its furry skin. Then men are happy to eat tinned bread, although it tastes like cardboard, if the fresh bread is no longer edible.

some 12,000 to 15,000 battle tanks, a resource which could have made a real impact on the land war. It is important to note that other methods for attacking allied shipping in the form of mines laid by surface vessels, surface raiders and aircraft attacks were equally successful and only just over 50% of allied shipping losses were attributed to U-boats. Of 5,219 allied ships lost during the course of the war with Germany only 2,827 were attributed to U-boat action.

The last things are brought on board. There is not much in the way of personal belongings, everything fits into a handbag, because underwear is seldom changed. The men sleep on board fully dressed, no-one can shave or even wash very often. Freshwater is also very valuable. A toothbrush and hand towel, perhaps a small picture for the locker, it can't be more than that. The Reich war flag is already waving on the tower's stern mast. The S.M.G against surprise air attacks is ready. The air vents above the tower, lead fresh air into the diesels as soon as they have been started.

In many respects this was a war that should never have been fought. In 1938, a series of war games and manoeuvres carried out by the Kriegsmarine had conclusively proven that the effective blockade of the British Isles would require an active force of 300 U-boats operating in the Atlantic. This figure was based on a loss rate to the U-boat force of 50%. When actual combat losses, boats in transit, boats under repair, training and construction were taken into consideration it was clear that in practice the U-boat force would have needed something like one thousand operational vessels to stand even the remotest prospect of success. The reality was that when war was declared the U-boat fleet amounted to just eleven training ships and 46 combat vessels. Of the combat craft, twenty were the small costal Type II boats and two were the unsuccessful Type I design, leaving a total force of just 24 ocean going U-boats ready for combat.

To begin the battle for the North Atlantic in 1939 with just 24 suitable combat ready boats was a futile mission. Although many more were under construction and the build programme was being hastily accelerated, the nine U-boats lost to enemy action in 1939 was proportionately a very heavy cross to bear and heralded the nightmare to come. The vanishingly slight chances of success for the U-boats in the beginning declined ever more rapidly as anti-submarine measures grew more efficient and deadly. There were simply never enough U-boats to achieve the strategic objective of choking the British Isles and the high command of the Kreigsmarine knew this to be the case. As the war progressed, the addition of extra operational theatres in the South Atlantic, Arctic, Caribbean, Mediterranean and Far East stretched those thin resources beyond the point where even the faintest hope of strategic success remained.

On land the Wehrmacht achieved some strategic successes, but after 1942 these were in short supply. In retrospect one of the main values of the U-boat fleet was to bolster a propaganda effort which gave false hope to the hard pressed German people. The exploits of the U-boats made a great story for cinema news reels, propaganda magazines and newspapers. The sea wolves were glamorised and hero worshipped. In order to feed the relentless appetite for success stories many U-boats were accompanied by film and photo journalists from the PK propaganda companies (Propaganda Kompanie), one of whom was Lothar–Gunther Buchheim, famous as the author of 'Das Boot', the fictionalised account of a journey which the writer as a PK member had undertaken in U96.

Over the six years of World War Two over 1200 U-boats were actually commissioned into the Kreigsmarine. Of these 731 were lost in combat and the inescapable fact is that never at any time did the losses they inflicted equate to the rate at which new allied ships were being built. The pressures of the uneven struggle grew worse as the war progressed. A U-boat was a complex vessel to sail which needed experienced handling, but as experienced crews were lost in the remorseless jaws of combat, less and less experienced crews were being sent to sea. From mid 1943 these boats were frequently being lost on their very first mission without ever having had the chance to strike a blow and a disconcertingly high number appear to have been lost to crew error. Some 52 U-boats are recorded as missing in action. Inevitably a number of these boats will have been lost to enemy action or mechanical failure but a substantial number are thought to lie on the bottom of the ocean as a result of inexperienced crews making fatal errors in the handling of these unforgiving craft.

All of the images and captions in this book are taken from the original wartime publication 'U-boot Auf Feindfahrt' published in 1942.

PRELIMINARY OBSERVATIONS

1 - In war, only submarine commanders who possess distinctive tactical knowledge and ability will be successful in the long run. In order, however, to understand and master the tactics (i.e., of submarine warfare), it is necessary to be thoroughly familiar with the weapon, and its characteristics and peculiarities; for it is on these that the tactics depend.

In addition, complete success as a result of a thorough exploitation of the possibilities of the weapon can only be achieved if all the officers in charge of it are trained to think along the same tactical lines.

The theoretical knowledge of the weapon, and of the appropriate tactics, must be supplemented, in the last resort, by the decisive requirement of a war-like spirit and an audacious outlook. The essence of submarine warfare is the offensive! For the commander of a submarine, therefore, the maxim: "He who wants to be victorious on the sea must always attack!" has special meaning.

2 - The following instructions, in which the experiences gained in the present war have been used, are concerned with the characteristics and uses of the submarines at present at our disposal, namely of submarines for torpedo attack.

The formulation of tactical rules for other types of submarines (artillery carrying submarines, mine-laying submarines) will only be possible when some experience has been gained of these types of vessel.

"Cast off bow and stern!" The commander during the casting off manoeuvre.

ck Out Receipt

urn - Seymour Public Library
-252-2571
p://www.seymourlibrary.org

day, January 5, 2015 7:47:01 PM
14

m: A30001130651
le: The official U-boat commanders handbook
: 01/26/2015

al items: 1

ing soon:
rning Backpacks in the Children's Room!

SECTION I
GENERAL

a) Essential Characteristics and Uses of the Submarine

3 - The chief characteristic and strength of the submarine is its invisibility due to its ability to submerge. As a consequence, the submarine is distinguished, at the same time, by another special feature, the advantage of surprise.

4 - The characteristic of invisibility serves both as a means of attack and a means of protection, and thus forms the basis for the naval use and suitability of the submarine:

  a. The underwater torpedo attack without warning, in daylight and on light nights during a full moon.
  b. The underwater night torpedo attack.
  c. The gunnery action and bombardment at night (only directed against unescorted single vessels in remote sea areas).
  d. The laying of mines (undetected).
  e. In short, the carrying out of independent operations in parts of the sea dominated by the enemy, where our own surface ships cannot operate.

5 - The most important naval task of our existing type of submarine is the undetected torpedo attack. This task imposes the upper limits of the size of the submarine, on the one hand because of the need for good general manoeuvrability, and on the other - having regard to the requirements of underwater warfare - because of the need for easy steering below the

surface. In contrast to other types of naval vessels, it is therefore not necessary to increase the size of submarines, to give them superiority over enemy vessels of the same category, since the attacks of submarines are directed against surface ships, usually much more powerful, whose offensive power is applied in a different way.

6 - If the size of the submarine is increased above these limits, in order, for example, to substitute for its proper use a greater suitability for minor (additional) operations, such as gunnery operations, its underwater fighting power is proportionately reduced. In that case, the ability of the submarine to go below the surface serves only as a protective measure, to enable it to evade the counteraction of the enemy.

7 - Compared with surface vessels of equal size, the submarine can stay a very long time at sea. In addition, its seaworthiness is unlimited, and it is in this respect in a stronger position than surface vessels of equal size. Both these considerations are of special importance in regard to its use in naval operations.

8 - As a result of the element of surprise by which it is characterized, the submarine - apart from direct naval successes which it is sought to obtain by its use - exercises a great influence on the military and strategical position, because the enemy must everywhere reckon with its appearance, and is influenced in a correspondingly high degree in his strategical decisions and military operations (detours, defensive measures, safety patrols, zigzag course).

9 - It must be required of the submarine that it shall be able to travel both on the surface and under water. For this purpose it requires two different systems of propulsion, the diesel motor for surface propulsion, and the "E" engine: electric motor

for underwater propulsion. The need for this dual propulsion system doubles the weight of the engines which the submarine is forced to carry, and entails a corresponding reduction of the performance of the individual propulsion unit. This is the cause of the relatively slow surface and underwater speeds of the submarine as compared with surface warships. This is the chief weakness of the submarine, which is of fundamental importance for its tactical use.

10 - Other weaknesses of the submarine are its restricted underwater radius of action, its low position in the water, and its great vulnerability.

11 - The weaknesses of the submarine must be offset by clever tactics, unscrupulous use, and obstinate persistence even when the chances of success appear slender.

The ropes are released and then coiled and stowed. The boat slowly moves away from the wharf and pushes into the current.

12 - Fundamentally, the part of the submarine in naval tactics is to operate alone, in accordance with its character and its principal task of carrying out, unseen, its annihilating attack on an adversary of considerably superior fighting strength.

13 - Consequently, there is no such thing as a concentration of submarines for the purpose of cooperating, and supporting one another, in a collective naval action.

A concentration of submarines can only have the object of a common tactical employment, but always without any distinct, close formal-tactical connection.

From the time the concentration goes into action, however, each submarine carries on the fight, as before, separately

The men stand on the upper deck wearing their worn "U-Boat parcels" and return the salute, whilst the strip of water between the boat and the wharf, where their comrades crowd together and wave, swells open wider and wider. The marching band that blasted out the farewell music, can still be seen and heard clearly, although the sound is half-swallowed by the howling wind: "Muss I denn, muss I denn ..." How long will the trip last? Will they bring many victory pennants back this time? Ah, just wait! The old man and us, we will do it alright!

and individually, although, in such circumstances, reciprocal indirect support, as, for example, by simultaneous attack, is possible.

14 - The principal task of the submarine, which is strong in attack and weak in defence, is the undetected, and therefore surprising, underwater or surface torpedo attack.

In no circumstances must the commander of the submarine allow his attention to be diverted, by lesser tasks, from this chief purpose, unless priority is expressly ordered to be given to other than offensive operations.

15 - During every attack, situations may develop in which a continuation of the attack appears to the submarine commander to be hopeless, or impossible. Only if the submarine commander, imbued with the determination to win, and unrelenting toward himself, conquers these feelings, will it be possible for him - in view of the few opportunities of attack which the war at sea will provide - to achieve any success at all.

16 - In all operations against the enemy, the commander of the submarine is entirely independent, and free to make his own decisions, unless special cooperation is called for.

Do not see danger everywhere and in everything, do not overestimate the enemy, do not always seek to place yourself in his position, do not assume that everything that is going on in the theatre of war applies to yourself these internal reservations and scruples are a sign of uncertainty, and of a negative attitude, which impairs your ability to reach a decision, and endangers the success of the operations.

Audacity and a readiness to take responsibility, coupled with cool, clear thinking, are the pre-conditions and the basis of success.

17 - Free

(Paragraphs marked "free" are those left open for future additions under the particular subject heading where they are found.)

18 - Free

b) How to Prevent the Submarine from Attracting Attention

19 - The chief value of the submarine is its characteristic ability, which it possesses in an exceptional degree, to attack without being seen, and thus to achieve the element of surprise. The precondition of success is surprise. If the submarine is seen by the enemy, it is deprived of almost every chance of success. The commander of the submarine must therefore make every effort to preserve the paramount advantage of surprise, as far as it is at all possible.

20 - In order to remain undetected, before and during the attack, the submarine must be neither sighted, nor sound-located nor detected by ASDIC.

i) Action to be Taken by the Submarine, in Order not to be Spotted

21 - In every situation, both on passage (or approach) and in launching the attack, the submarine must be guided by the motto: "He who sees first, has won!" Untiring vigilance of the look-out involves success and safety of the submarine, and is, therefore, at one and the same time, a means of attack and defence.

Consequently, when operating on the surface, a sharp lookout should always be kept, systematically organized in sectors (examination of the horizon for ships, of the surrounding surface of the sea for periscopes, and of the sky for aircraft). The most dangerous enemy of the submarine is the aircraft, by reason of its great speed. Consequently, during daylight and on moonlit nights, the sky should be watched with special care.

22 - To keep a conscientious lookout is tiring; consequently, the look-out should be punctually and frequently relieved. Sunglasses should be held in readiness for all members of the watch.

Particular attention should be paid to the sun sector, in order to be safe from sudden air attack.

23 - The periscope should not be used in daylight, on the surface, except in special circumstances (for example, in remote sea areas; also as under No. 24. It is the raised periscope on the surface that makes the typical submarine silhouette. Similarly, on submerging in daylight, the periscope should not be raised until the submarine is well below the surface. In the same way, the submarine should not surface during the day, before the periscope has been lowered.

24 - If, for urgent reasons, such as overhauling, it should become imperatively necessary to raise the periscope by day when the submarine is on the surface, the additional height of the raised periscope can be used in suitable weather to send up a look-out with binoculars, provided that surprise attacks by hostile airplanes are not to be anticipated. If the weather is clear and the sea calm, advantage can be taken of the raising of the periscope, for an all-round view. On account of the relatively week magnification of the periscope, however, and of the almost inevitable vibrations and movement of the vessel, this seldom

serves a useful purpose. The danger of betraying oneself by the raised periscope is greater.

25 - In clear weather, do not allow yourself to be seen on the dip of the horizon. Submerge, at the latest, when the top of the funnel of the sighted ship is visible in the dip of the horizon. Some warships, besides having lookout posts with binoculars on the mast, have range finders of great optical efficiency in the foretop. In clear weather, therefore, one should never be able to see more of the enemy than the tops of his masts. Anyone who can see more - i.e., who approaches nearer - automatically runs the danger of being sighted, himself, by the enemy.

It is better to submerge too soon than too late, and thus lose one's chance altogether. The limits of what is possible in various kinds of weather can only be learned by experience. The look-out on merchant ships, and the danger of being sighted at night, are easily overestimated.

26 - If there is a danger of surprise attacks in sea areas efficiently patrolled by hostile planes and warships, and especially if the submarine is engaged in operations there that require it to be stationary, It must remain underwater from dawn to dusk.

27 - It may also be advisable to remain submerged in misty or foggy weather. In poor visibility, the approach of ships can be more easily detected underwater (from the sound of the ships' engines) by means of the hydrophone, than on the surface by the look-out.

28 - This possibility of using the hydrophone to help in detecting surface ships should, however, be restricted to those cases in which the submarine is unavoidably compelled to stay below the surface. The hydrophone must not lead to inactivity

(passivity) underwater, which would be wrong; it is an auxiliary instrument and no more, and can never be a substitute for ocular perception and surface viewing. As soon as visibility allows, the place of the submarine is on the surface. Otherwise valuable opportunities of attack are lost.

29 - The danger of a surprise attack exists, in particular, when the submarine comes to the surface, especially after travelling long distances at considerable depth. When coming up from a considerable depth, an all-round sound location should therefore be carried out at a safe depth, where the submarine cannot be rammed; i.e., at a depth of approximately 20m, at "sound-location speed." Next, the submarine should go rapidly through

The diesels then turn with more power, the engine telegraph rings and the boat glides more quickly out of the harbour towards the open Atlantic. The crew that is not on duty is on the upper deck. When the boat has passed the mined area, they will be ordered into the boat with the call, "Crew down from the upper deck!" Then, only the bridge watch will remain outside, four men for every four hours; at most, the commander as well. Otherwise, guests are only allowed if there is no alarm to be expected. No-one walks on the upper deck in the Atlantic. Some men will not see daylight during the entire operation.

the danger zone at periscope depth, with the periscope raised; careful all-round look-out with and without magnification -submersion up to 9m, depending on the weather, then lower the periscope altogether (see No. 23) and surface at high speed. The manhole of the conning tower is opened as quickly as possible, and the commander - with, at the most, one man who is especially good as a look-out - goes up. It is not until the surface of the sea has again been examined with binoculars, in every direction, that the compressed air cells can be completely emptied of water.

30 - By careful supervision, the submarine should be prevented from leaving traces of oil (leaking oil tanks, etc.). Patches of oil may also be left behind when submerging, as a result of a residue of air in the compressed air cells. Consequently, the submarine should not remain near the place where it has submerged.

The wide Atlantic rocks the tiny boat up and down beneath the vast bell of the heavens. Four men keep an untiring watch on the open bridge. The success and safety of the entire boat is largely in their hands.

31 - After the submarine has submerged, the periscope can be shown in a low position, and left there, up to a distance of approximately 4 to 5,000m from the enemy, according to the state of the weather.

At lesser distances, the "sparing" use of the periscope begins, that is to say, the periscope is frequently and intermittently shown, each time for a little while, in a very low position where it is almost always awash, while the submarine travels at low speed.

For rules for the use of the periscope when attacking, see Section II, C, No. 125.

32 - For the colour of the periscope, a dull, dirty grey such as is used for the body of the submarine itself should be chosen, as this colour is the least easy to detect in all conditions of light. Green paint, or stripes or checkered patterns, are very conspicuous in a poor light.

33 - Every aircraft sighted should be regarded as hostile until the contrary is proved.

34 - Submarines on the surface are not easily detected from an aircraft when the sea is rough, unless seen in their characteristic outline against the dip of the horizon. If the sea is calm, the track (wake) of the submarine is usually seen first from the plane, especially if the submarine is moving at speed.

35 - The submarine must endeavour to keep a sufficiently sharp look-out to be able to see the aircraft before it is spotted by .the latter. It is then master of the situation, and will soon learn to decide whether it must submerge, or can remain on the surface; If it is not certain that the latter can be done, it is better to reduce the chances of success by a premature temporary submersion, or

a retreat to greater depths to avoid being spotted by the aircraft, than to spoil the chance altogether by being spotted.

36 - In good visibility, it is possible to sight the plane in time. It is consequently right to remain on the surface in areas threatened from the air and to keep the area under observation. More can be seen above water than below. In addition, by remaining below, valuable opportunities of attack may be lost.

37 - Conditions are different, in particular, in areas threatened from the air when the submarine is engaged in operations that cause it to remain stationary in misty weather, with poor visibility .and low clouds. In such circumstances it is right to remain submerged during the day, because, if it has surfaced, the submarine may easily be surprised by aircraft suddenly appearing in near sight, without being able to submerge in time, and reach safety.

38 - The submerged submarine is most difficult to spot from the plane when all its horizontal surfaces are painted very dark. All other bright objects on the upper deck, as, for example, the insulators on the net wire, must have a coating of dark paint. In case of need, paint Which has crumbled, or been washed off during the operations, must be replaced; for this purpose, a quantity of dark paint should always be available during operations.

39 - A submarine painted in this way can only be spotted by an airplane, if the submarine is submerged:
    a. When the sun is shining, and the sunlight penetrates the water below the surface; without the sun, the water is a dark mass, which hides all objects from view.
    b. When the surface of the sea is not so rough -

approximately from motion. (sea) 2 to 3 upwards - that the continuous refraction makes it impossible to see below the surface, even when the sun is shining.

c. When the airplane is almost vertically above the submarine. Because of the high speed of the airplane, it is very difficult to spot a submarine moving under water.

The conditions described above - sun, rough sea, position of the aircraft in relation to the submerged submarine - are relatively more favourable or unfavourable for the airplanes in sea areas with exceptionally clear, or exceptionally turbid, water, for example, in the Mediterranean, and in the Baltic at the mouths of rivers. In sea areas where the water is clear, so that it is correspondingly easier to look into it from airplanes directly above, the submarine must therefore submerge, in good time, to a greater depth, in order not to be spotted.

40 - Even when the submarine is not travelling at speed, if the sea is smooth, the tracks (wake) of the screw (propeller) of the vessel, and of the periscope, may betray the submarine to the airplane. When there is a danger of air attack in such conditions, the submarine should therefore submerge in good time - diving to a considerable depth, except when the sky is kept under observation through the periscope.

41 - What to do incase of air attack: see Nos. 266 to 270.

42 - Free

43 - Free

44 - Free

45 - Free

ii) Principles of Defence by Means of Sound Location

46 - The underwater torpedo attack of the submarine without warning is bound up with defence against sound location of the enemy.

The efficiency of the enemy sound location depends on:
    a. The efficiency of the sound locator (hydrophone).
    b. The acoustical conductivity of the water.
    c. The interference level of the sound-locating vessel.
    d. The volume of the sound to be located.

47 - The efficiency of the various types of enemy sound locators (hydrophones) is not known. In estimating it, we can assume that it is similar to that of our own sound locating instruments.

48 - The acoustical conductivity of the water depends on the uniformity of its condition. Differences of temperature and salt content - that is to say, in the different layers of the water - which are caused by currents, tides, and the motion of the sea - reduce the conductivity of the water. The same result is brought about by permeation of the water with air, or with plankton containing air. Uniformly high or uniformly low temperatures, as well as uniformly high or uniformly low proportions of salt in the water, increase the conductivity. In the Baltic and the North Sea, conditions are generally bad for sound locating; in other words, favourable for submarines.

49 - The interference level of the sound-locating vessel depends on the magnitude of the sounds proceeding from it, and on the state of the sea. Travelling at speed, and rough seas, as well as the proximity of other ships, greatly impair the efficiency of the sound locating instruments.

50 - The magnitude of the sounds originating in the submerged

They stand there hour after hour; the watch officer on the bow starboard side, the bo'sun on the port side, and at the stern the two lookouts in the crew. Hour after hour they check the horizon, the sky, the sea, for enemy "colleagues", attacking aircraft; for pursuers and for booty. Every man has his own 90 degree sector. The periscope mounting gives good stability. Between it and the bridge covering is a good place to hold the glasses up to your eyes if your hands are free. Keeping watch, keeps you alive! The area beneath the curve of the horizon has to be considered: for slim masts and pale wisps of smoke that the naked eye can't make out; they rise up above the separating curve, one just has to find them!

submarine can be greatly reduced by travelling at "sound location speed." The degree of speed most favourable for sound location, and the magnitudes of the sounds originating in the individual machines, engines (motors), and instruments, may be different in each individual boat, and must be determined by sound locating tests. The procedure appropriate to each submarine, when travelling at "sound location speed", must be determined by the result of these tests.

    a. Low speed: the revolutions must in this case be determined by the sound locating tests, and must in certain circumstances be different for each screw.

    b. Maximum silence of the crew in the submarine; speaking in low tones, working noiselessly; all auxiliary machines, etc., stopped, as far as they can be dispensed with (see also Section IV, A, No. 250).

In our waters, with their usually irregular layers, a submarine travelling at "sound location speed" can in general hardly be detected even by a slowly moving vessel pursuing it by sound location. In parts of the ocean with a better acoustic conductivity, conditions are more favourable for the enemy; in such sea areas the submarine should therefore take all precautions when travelling at "sound location speed."

What to do when being pursued by sound location: see Section IV, A, Nos. 250 to 257.

51 - Free
52 - Free
53 - Free
54 - Free

iii) Principles of Position Finding (ASDIC)

55 - To enable the underwater torpedo attack to be carried out

without warning, It is further necessary that the submarine shall not be located by ASDIC.

The premises of the efficiency of the enemy defence based on ASDIC are the same as for sound location (see Nos. 46 to 54), viz.:

    a. The efficiency of the submarine detecting gear.

    b. The conditions for ASDIC resulting from the capacity of the water for transmitting the waves (rays) of the echo sounder.

    c. The interference level of the hunting vessel.

    d. The size of the echo-sounding surface of the target.

56 - The efficiency of enemy submarine detecting gear cannot yet be finally judged by experience so far gained during the war. It appears, however, that we have to reckon with submarine detecting gear of a performance equal to that of our "S" equipment.

This U-Boat officer of the watch, seems like a descendant of the ancient Viking sea kings from the era of Germanic seafarers.

a. The success of the ASDIC operations depends on the strength of the echo. Experience gamed with our "S" equipment shows that the volume of the echo depends on the depth reached by the submerged target of the ASDIC operations? and that it frequently decreases in proportion as the depth of the target increases. In certain cases it will therefore be possible, by intercepting the enemy's echo impulses, and observing their strength (amplitude), to determine the most favourable depth. The weaker the reception of the echo impulses, the weaker the echo received by the enemy.

b. The echo impulses can be heard with both the "Hand K.D.B." and the "G.H.G." ("G" Sound Locator and/or "G" Hydrophone). In the case of the "G.H.G.," the high frequency filter should be used; that is to say, low sound frequencies should be cut out.

Between the two lookouts on bridge watch astern, are the retracted periscope and the freely-hanging bridge compass. The man on the port side is cleaning the lenses of his binoculars; they get sprayed even on such an apparently bright and peaceful day.

c. According to the experiences so far gained of the acoustical perception of the enemy's submarine detecting gear, we have to reckon with different kinds of echo impulses: in part, similar impulses to those of our own "S" equipment, but deeper in tone, in part, a constant humming. On several occasions, both sounds were audible, not only in the sound locator (hydrophone) but also everywhere in the vessel. Other experiences show that the enemy echo impulses resemble the ticking of a dock, or the tone of the "Atlas" echo sounder, and in other cases a tone increasing and decreasing in volume, which is a good direction finding target (bearing target), or that they resemble metallic blows on the sides of the submarine. Among the manifestations of sound which resemble those of our "S" equipment, an interval of the impulses of 7 seconds has several times been unmistakably observed.

d. According to the experience so far gained, and the reports received, the submarine detecting gear used by the enemy seems, more especially, to supply exact particulars of depth.

57 - As regards the conditions of ASDIC in relation to the transmitting capacity of the water, it has been ascertained that the efficiency of the submarine-detecting gear is considerably reduced in sea areas with numerous layers of water.

a. Formation of layers of varying density ("stratification") of the water of the sea occurs after a long spell of sunshine on a calm sea, and also in a high degree in places where there is a mingling of different kinds of water, for example, at the confluence of the brackish waters of the Baltic with the salt water of the North Sea, in the Skagerrak and Kattegat; also in the Straits of

Gibraltar, and on the confines of the Gulf Stream, in the Gulf Stream itself, near the mouths of rivers, and in other places (see Atlas of Water Densities of the Oceans). These "stratifications" of the water bring about a deflection of the wave of the echo sounder, so that the echo does not return to the receiver. In these circumstances, the submarine detecting gear does not function at all, or only for very short distances. According to this, it is to be assumed, that the submarine detecting equipment of the enemy is frequently less efficacious in summer than in winter, and that this also applies to waters with a marked "stratification" (Skagerrak, Kattegat, West Coast of Norway, Pentland Firth, vicinity of the Gulf Stream, Straits of Gibraltar). Continual observation and measuring of water densities and temperatures are therefore important and indispensable, for establishing the presence of "stratification" when submerging to considerable depths as a means of evading pursuit by position finding.

b. In addition, position finding is very difficult, and almost impossible, in shallow water of varying depths (sand banks), where there are many wrecks, as well as in narrow bays (Norwegian fjords), as it is usually not an echo that is produced, but numerous echoes, which make it difficult to keep, but more especially to locate, the target.

58 - The interference level of the hunting vessel is determined - also in hydrophone (sound locator) reception - by its wake, and by the state of the sea. High speed of the hunting vessel, and rough seas, limit the efficiency of the submarine detecting gear, or make it impossible to get results, because of the extensive permeation of the water with air in the neighbourhood of the

ship. For this reason, the conditions for hunting are usually unfavourable in the stern sector of the hunting vessel, as a result of the disturbance of the water by the propeller.

59 - The size of the echo-sounding surface of the target is of decisive importance for the strength of the echo.

    a. If the submarine is broadside on in relation to the hunting ship, it will be more easily located than when it shows the narrow silhouette. Consequently, it is a matter of principle to show the narrow silhouette when being pursued by ASDIC. It is then, generally

The grey leathers, known as the "U-Boat parcel", also keep you warm and deflect a lot of water. If the distance is smeared with cloud and rain, then you have to be twice as careful. Nothing should get past us in our sector. The fast, lone vessels have to be found and attacked too and destroyed if possible, difficult as that may be; not just the slower, well-protected convoys that announce themselves from a distance.

speaking, and as long as the submarine is not travelling at speed, immaterial whether the bows or the stern are turned toward the pursuer. The narrow silhouette over the bows is better, because, in the forward direction, the conditions are more advantageous for the submarine in regard to sound location by direction finding (bearing) and observation of echo impulses.

b.   The behaviour of the submarine when pursued by ASDIC is in other respects dictated by the same principles as apply to pursuit by sound location, viz.: maximum silence on board, since the submarine detecting gear is, or may be, suitable for use as a receiver for the ASDIC impulses.

Regarding other action to be taken in case of pursuit by the ASDIC method, see Section IV, B, Nos. 254 to 257.

60 - Free
61 - Free
62 - Free
63 - Free
64 - Free

c) Use of the Means of Communication of the Submarine

65 - The only means of communication between the submarine and Headquarters, and between the submarines themselves, which is of decisive importance for the development and success of the attack, is wireless telegraphy. The permanent supervision of the execution of orders, and of the observance of the rules for the communications service, devolves on the officer is charge of the wireless communications service of the submarine.

The communications service is subject to the provisions of

the N.V.II (Wireless Service), and to the rules of communication of the "Permanent War (Service) Orders of the Commander in Chief of Submarines" ("B.d.U.") as a supplement, which are kept up to date in accordance with the latest information.

A thorough knowledge of these orders, on the part of the commander, the officer of the watch, and the wireless personnel, is a precondition for an adequate and efficient operation of the communications service.

Reception

66 - By frequent repetition of the wireless messages, by selection of suitable short waves, and by the use of maximum wave transmitters, the greatest care must be taken to enable each submarine to pick up each message.

The submarine, on its part, must do everything in its power to pick up as soon as possible the wireless messages transmitted according to an agreed plan.

Transmission

67 - By transmitting a wireless message, the submarine always exposes itself to the danger of being located by direction finding. This circumstance must not, however, deter the submarine from transmitting messages that are of importance for Headquarters and the other submarines.

Important messages

68 - Important messages are:
    a. Enemy reports which make it possible to send other submarines into action.
    b. Warnings referring to the positions of enemy submarines or minefields. (No reports about single drifting mines, unless they give a clue to hitherto unknown or unsuspected mine fields or "mine contamination.")

c. Reports on the situation in the theatre of operation, traffic, possible use of armed forces, description and strength of patrols.

d. Weather reports.

e. Position (station) and reports on movements of ships, insofar as the transmission of these reports is required by Headquarters, or seems necessary to enable them to assess the position.

f. Reports called for by Headquarters. What reports are required is stated in the operation order.

The commander on the bridge observes, hour after hour, the enemy convoy that they are following. They have to keep their nerve, use every chance, tenacious and decisive, to guess the enemy's thoughts, their course, and determine in advance their intentions. They must evade their defences, without allowing themselves to be driven aside, noticed, or forced under water. Then the contact will be lost and everything was in vain. And if they are discovered prematurely, then there are depth charges instead of success. U-Boat bread is hard as bones!

Short Signals

69 - A large proportion of the messages can be transmitted by means of short signals, which experience has shown to reduce to a minimum the danger of being located by direction finding.

When to Transmit Messages

70 - Messages for the transmission of which no special time has been fixed should be transmitted, as far as possible, in the evening or during the night, and before important changes of position, in order to frustrate a possible reaction of the enemy to a bearing by sending into action antisubmarine formations or aircraft, or by diverting ships or convoys.

Reporting Position of Submarine

71 - Each message must include a report of the position of the submarine.

Danger of Location by D/F

72 - The enemy probably has at his disposal, at least in his homeland, a well-developed and efficient D/F (direction-finding) system. As the waves emanating from the submarine are speedily detected by the spotting service of the enemy, the possibility must always be reckoned with that a number of suitable stations are ready to take bearings.

The quality of a bearing depends -leaving out of consideration the conditions of reception -mainly on the length of the beam, and on the angle of intersection of several beams.

Near the English coast, the direction-finding of a wireless message of medium length will in most cases result in a fairly exact location of the position of the submarine. In the English channel and the adjoining sea areas, in the approaches to the Pentland Firth, and east and west of the Orkneys, special precautions should be taken, as, in these areas, the danger exists of an immediate action carried out by anti-submarine vessels and aircraft following the D/F location of the position of a submarine or submarines. In more remote sea areas (more than 200 km from the coast) an immediate reaction to a D/F operation is hardly to be anticipated.

The shorter the message, the more inaccurate the bearing.

Short signals are attended in a lesser degree by the danger of D/F location, but the possibility must also be reckoned with.

73 - Free
74 - Free

d) Limits of the Uses of the Submarine

75 - The duration of the operational use of the submarine is limited by the time it can remain at sea (fuel, victualling), and by the efficiency of the commander and crew. Apart is also played by the nature of the operations (mine laying operations, etc., in close proximity to a heavily guarded enemy coast, or operations against merchant shipping on the high seas) and the efficacy of the relative enemy countermeasures during the operations.

76 - It cannot be assumed that submarines operating in the face of strong enemy counter-pressure will be able to stay long at their allotted positions. It must be left to the commander to decide when and for how long he judges a break to be necessary (shearing off, lying on the bottom, travelling at low depths).

77 - The operational speed of submarines engaged in invisible war operations decreases in proportion as enemy counteraction in the deployment of air and sea forces, and by other means, is intensified. It is also affected by the state of the sea, the duration of daylight, and other factors.

Consequently, the speed at which long-distance operations are carried out can only be roughly estimated. If the utmost economy is practiced, the operational speed of small submarines will not exceed 5 to 6 knots; that of medium-sized and large submarines will not be more than 6 to 7 knots.

78 - A rough state of the sea restricts the use of submarines as a weapon of war:

    a. As regards the underwater use of torpedoes: as soon as the underwater steering gear can no longer be controlled

It is a great opportunity for the German boats that they are so difficult to see. They are hardly distinguishable from the sea that washes over them. They don't form a silhouette against the sky, especially not at night. On the other hand, the disadvantage of their low height is that one cannot see across very large areas, which is possible from the mast of a larger vessel; and one is constantly wet, even in a light swell. In bad weather the water even comes in, the ocean pure, especially when the swell is running behind the boat. Many men have been washed overboard, even if attached with a safety line. U-Boat men are hard men. They are trained to become hard and proud, through the battle with nature in which a man has to assert himself, and in fighting the enemy.

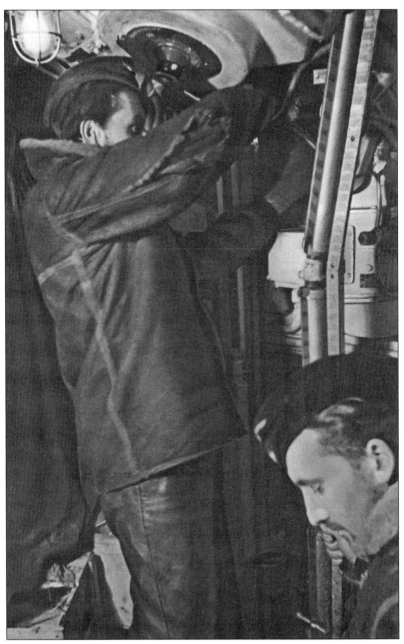

The time has come. After long and careful observation of the enemy, the boat has got ahead of it. The attack is started. It dives. The petty officer operates the flooding vents in the control room. The boat is kept floating according to instructions from the C.E. at the depth ordered by the commander.

at periscope depth. In the case of small submarines, the dividing line will be sea No. 5 or 6, for medium and large boats, sea No. 6 or 7, approximately.

b. As regards the surface use of torpedoes: the dividing line in this case is reached in somewhat less rough conditions than apply to the underwater use of torpedoes, on account of the unfavourable influence of the rough sea on the manoeuvrability of the vessel on the surface.

c. As regards the use of gunnery: as soon as it becomes impossible to man the gun.

79 - If the operations are carried out at a depth of 20m and less, the loss of the submarine must be reckoned with, once it has been detected. But in such cases also, as has been demonstrated by the experience gained in wartime, difficult situations due to pursuit by the enemy may well be mastered, if the commander acts cleverly and coolly, and the crew remains steadfast ("U 9" in the spring of 1940, "U 123," "U 333" in the spring of 1942).

Submarines should not in general be used at depths of less than 16m.

80 - Free
81 - Free
82 - Free
83 - Free
84 - Free
85 - Free
86 - Free
87 - Free
88 - Free
89 - Free
90 - Free

SECTION II
THE UNDERWATER TORPEDO ATTACK

a) Fundamental Rules for the Underwater Attack

91 - The object of the underwater attack is to discharge a torpedo with the certainty of hitting, but without warning, and at short range. The shorter the distance between the submarine and the target, the more reliable the assessment of the speed, course, and position of the enemy. The torpedo attack at short range is the most advantageous also because not even important miscalculations affecting the launching of the missile can take effect to any appreciable extent, on account of the short course of the torpedo, and by reason of the fact that any counter-action on the part of the enemy - for example, a change of course (evading), if the submarine or the torpedo is spotted - comes too late.

92 - The lower limit of the torpedo attack at dose range is defined by the distance needed to set the torpedo on its course at the appropriate depth, and by the safety interval, i.e., the distance of the submarine from the point of detonation of the torpedo. No torpedo attack should, therefore, be carried out at a range under 300m.

93 - Invisibility during the attack is made possible by the judicious, invisible use of the periscope, the surgeless launching of the torpedo, and the absence of bubbles in the track of the torpedo.

94 - The efficiency of the sound-locating and ASDIC equipment of the enemy is dependent on the state of the sea, the nature of the water (i.e., conditions of "stratification," etc.), the speed of the enemy (see Section I, B, II and III), the attentiveness of the personnel, and other factors. The danger to be anticipated from the sound location and ASDICs of the enemy should not be allowed to prevent the carrying out of a fatal attack at short range.

95 - When attacking ships with low and medium speeds, at close range, it is ballistically advantageous to fire at an angle of the target of 90, as errors in estimating the position will in this case have the least effect, besides which the speed of the enemy can be most accurately gauged in this position. If the range is longer (over 1,000m), and the target is travelling at a high rate of speed, an attempt should be made to launch the torpedo at a smaller angle, say, 60.

96 - The method of carrying out the attack is based, as long as range finding with subsequent deflection (change of bearing) measuring (keeping the reckoning) is not practicable, on the particulars of the enemy characteristics obtained by the viewing method during the preparation of the underwater attack, or on the estimates of the enemy characteristics obtained underwater: position, speed, range. The estimation of the characteristics of the target from the level of the submarine, and with the aid of the monocular optical system of the periscope, is difficult, and requires continual thorough practice.

97 - The estimation of the position is easiest when the submarine stations itself forward of the beam. If the sun is behind the target, the assessment of the position is difficult.

The diesels have been switched off for the dive. It is quiet in the boat, suddenly oddly quiet. The petty officer in the e-room operates the switch to transfer to the electric motor; because under water, it delivers the power, the diesels need air! All orders are given via the engine telegraph, as they are above water for the diesel crew. It warns with a sharp ring, its pointer sets out the ordered speed. In the same way, the petty officer gets his readings from it and reports that the actions have been carried out.

98 - The speed of the enemy can best be calculated from the position forward of the beam. In calculating the speed, attention should be paid to the water at the stern rather than to the sea near the bows, because, if the shape of the bows is narrow (pointed), the visible effect of the progress of the ship is often very slight. In addition, it is more difficult to camouflage the stern (i.e., so as to create the impression of movement, etc.).

In estimating the enemy's speed, his course in relation to the direction of the waves, as well as the change of bearing, should be taken into consideration.

99 - Every available opportunity should be taken of practicing range finding (i.e., estimating the range). In estimating ranges, conditions of visibility play an important part. In dear weather, and with the sun behind one's back, the distance is liable to be underestimated, in poor visibility, against the sun, in conditions of twilight (dusk and dawn), and by moonlight, to be overestimated.

100 - Favourable conditions for attack.

    a. With the sun behind: The torpedo control officer (the officer in charge of the discharging of the torpedoes) is not dazzled, but can clearly see the sharp outline of the target. From the enemy ship, the periscope, raised no more than is absolutely necessary, is not to be seen among the reflections of the bright sun in the water; and also a trail of bubbles can not usually be seen until it is too late.

    b. From the weather side (windward). The periscope should move with the sea. The waves, coming from behind, always wash over a periscope which is in the right position, that is to say, in a low position; and the splashes and spray water of the periscope are not easily made out. In addition, the enemy look-out to windward, especially in a strong wind, or in heavy rain, meets with difficulties. As regards the weather side (windward), if the wind is moderate, torpedoes discharged from the stern form an exception (i.e., to the above), inasmuch as the submarine, in moving with the waves (that is, in this case to leeward) comes near to riding on the waves, whereas to windward driving against the sea - the periscope may cause conspicuous splashes even when the submarine is travelling at low speed. In a keen wind, however, the windward side is also more favourable for the stern launching of torpedoes, because the enemy, as a matter of course, then keeps a better lookout to leeward, and observation is better.

c. Wind 3 to 4 and sea 2 to 3 are most favourable for making the attack, because the sea then washes over the low-lying periscope, without interfering with the view of the target, while the action of the underwater (depth) steering gear is not adversely affected.

101 - Unfavourable conditions for attack.

a. Heavy seas or swell: It is difficult to keep the submarine at the right depth for attack, especially when the attack has to be carried out against the sea. According to the qualities (efficiency) of the underwater steering gear of the boat, this will soon put a limit to the possibilities of underwater attack (see Section I, D, No. 78). It is in a rough sea that an attack in a direction parallel to the waves is more likely to succeed most favourable for the underwater steering of the submarine and the depth course of the torpedo).

b. Sea as smooth as oil: The slightest ripple even of the low periscope is noticeable, and easily observable by

The chief engineer ordered, "One hundred litres, deballast". The control room seaman turns the vent and the electrically-operated pumps start to hum. When the control gauge shows that the required amount of water has flowed through, the man abruptly cuts off the stream by closing the valve. He reports the final reading on the gauge, "One hundred litres have been pumped out!".

the enemy. Exceptions: enemy coming out of a bright sun; conditions of twilight; moonlit nights.

c. Attack with dark thunderclouds in the background; even the most efficiently camouflaged (painted) periscope will then appear white against the dark black clouds.

d. Against the sun: the estimation of speed, position and distance (range) is considerably more difficult; besides which, if the attack is carried out against the sun, there is the danger of attracting attention by the flashes of light proceeding from the objective (lens system of the periscope).

102 - Free

103 - Free

104 - Free

b) Preparing for the Underwater Attack

105 - General rules for the attack:

a. The submarine commander should be alert and suspicious on patrol, as long as there is no target; but everything should be thrown into the attack.

b. Proceed with care when a target has been found. The attack should be carried out with indomitable resolution and steadfastness, until final success, resulting in the annihilation of the enemy, has been achieved. During the attack, situations often arise which would be a reason for disengaging from the enemy. These moments of doubt, and these temptations, must be conquered.

c. Never delude yourself by assuming that it is right not to attack on the instant, or not to hold on the enemy with the utmost determination, because there may be reason to hope and believe that a better target will subsequently be found elsewhere. What you have got, you have got. Do not let such considerations give you the idea of trying to save fuel.

d. The attack should only be postponed in case of imperative necessity, for example at dusk - if it should already be too dark for underwater torpedo launching - in order to be able to carry out a surface attack after night-fall, with greater safety and a better chance of success.

e. In every submarine attack, whether by day or by night, the attempt must be made to obtain reliable data for aiming (controlling) the torpedo, by exhausting all possibilities with care and deliberation (measuring the deflection with the aid of the line (of the horizon), increase the size of the masts at a given height in the 1/16 scale, overhauling as to course and speed, by day and night, on the surface). Do not attack immediately at random; success cannot be achieved that way.

f. Do not attack from positions which offer no chance of success. Keep your head and wait, in order - in daytime, if it is still light enough - to make a second attack by another overhauling manoeuvre, or in order to attack at night.

g. Particularly difficult objectives for the submarine are: destroyers, on account of their speed and the relative shortness of the target they offer, and submarines, on account of their small height (difficulty of range finding), and their shape above water, which is unfavourable for estimating their position. Consequently, attacks on destroyers and submarines can only be carried out at short range. No single shots; "fan" shooting.

h. In wartime, one is always farther away from the enemy than one thinks, especially at night. Hold out, then; and go near. Firing at close range also makes for greater safety for your own boat. In the neighbourhood of its own ships the enemy escort will not at first drop depth charges.

106 - As a matter of principle, every underwater attack should be so prepared and carried out that the launching of torpedoes can take place at the earliest possible moment. Favourable

The commander has ordered, "Keep the boat exactly at periscope depth!".
In a sea swell, that is not easy. Above the backs of the two helmsmen, the C.E.
(chief engineer) at the controls, observes the boat's position exactly. He lets
several litres flood in or be pumped out or regulated accordingly, (he has it
pumped forwards or to the rear) and has the positions of the bow, stern or
depth rudders altered.

opportunities of attack may be lost by hesitating. If conditions allow, the submarine should therefore go to meet the enemy. It is wrong to keep ahead of the enemy and wait until he comes into range.

107 - The commander must be quick, resolute and versatile, and be guided by circumstances in deciding which method of attack is the most favourable, and will most quickly achieve success. As long as the enemy is in range, the submarine must be in a position to launch a torpedo at any moment, in case the enemy takes counter-measures, by veering, etc., even if the desired position most favourable for launching the attack, for example, an angle of 90, has not yet been reached. The commander should never concentrate rigidly and schematically on a certain desired position, and operate with that exclusive object in view.

108 - On account of the low underwater speed of the submarine, a position forward of the beam of the enemy is a necessity when making the underwater attack proper. The initial position for the underwater attack must be the more forward of the enemy's beam, the greater the distance is between the submarine and the enemy. In normal visibility and normal conditions of attack, the submarine should therefore not dive for the underwater attack until it has reached the position 0 in relation to the general course of the enemy.

109 - If the submarine is not already ahead of the enemy's beam when the latter comes in sight, an attempt must be made to reach the required position at top speed on the surface. The most favourable converging course in relation to the enemy when overhauling, is always the course vertical to the sight bearing, as long as the submarine is in a more forward position than abreast of the enemy.

110 - In taking up its station forward to the beam of the enemy, the submarine must not endanger its most valuable asset, invisibility. In daytime, in clear weather, the submarine should not therefore be able to see more of the enemy than just the tops of his masts (look-out on the mast, range-finder in the foretop, see Section I, B, No. 25).

111 - Attention should be paid to the differences in the conditions of visibility of the various sea areas. Conditions can be encountered in which it is possible to approach much nearer to a surface ship, without immediately being spotted, because the air is not always absolutely clear, and the dip of the horizon is frequently blurred and misty. In the Atlantic a submarine can be spotted by the enemy as soon as it is lifted by the swell of the sea - as occasionally happens - even when, for a considerable length of time, the submarine could not previously have been visible from the enemy ship.

112 - The overhauling manoeuvre requires a high degree of tactical ability; its success is the pre-condition of the following underwater attack, and therefore the success of the operation. As a tactical masterpiece, the overhauling manoeuvre is therefore the exclusive business of the commander, and its preparation and execution require his unremitting attention.

113 - In fighting its way forward to the position ahead of the be am of the enemy, in borderline conditions of visibility during the day, the submarine is engaged in a long, drawn-out and extremely tiring overhauling operation. It is an incessant "nibbling at the horizon" (i.e., to keep the enemy on the dip of the horizon) - going in again and again as soon as the tops of the masts get smaller, and sheering off again at once, as soon as they rise higher again. These strenuous efforts to overhaul

the enemy are continued, in the Atlantic, hour by hour, and can only succeed as a result of indomitable resolution and an unchanging, obstinate refusal to let the enemy escape, even when the submarine finds that progress is very slow. Any change of course on the part of the enemy, or engine trouble, etc., occurring on board the enemy ship, may immediately alter the position in favour of the submarine.

The helmsmen for the depth rudder, sit in front of their buttons. They observe the boat's changing weight distribution, which is shown in the spirit level. Afterwards, they operate the upwards and downwards buttons. If a break in the electrical current occurs, they operate a large hand wheel for positioning the rudder. All around, there is a confusing amount of equipment; the valves and pressure gauges of the control room, this heart chamber of the submarine.

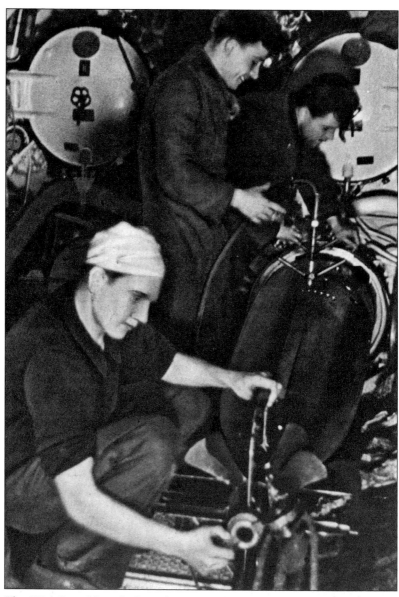

The "Eels" – although their shape is rather more like a mackerel – have to be constantly checked. They are not projectiles like shells, but rather, according to the calibration, independent, self-steering little vessels with a live detonation head. Dynamite carriers. The torpedoman's mate and his two mechanic seamen, the "mixers", have the job of maintaining them. They are just "pulling the eel": the torpedo has been pulled halfway out of the tube in which it lies – secured, but otherwise ready to fire – and is being "cared for".

114 - The overhauling manoeuvre should always be exploited, in order to obtain the particulars of the enemy (course, speed, pattern of the zigzag course) by careful observation of the course of the submarine itself, exact D/F of the enemy ship, estimation of range and position at regular intervals of time. These particulars are almost always more reliable than those obtained underwater.

115 - The overhauling manoeuvre and the attack should not be abandoned even when the bearing shows little movement of the enemy. Do not let the difficulties wear you down!

116 - Free

117 - Whether or not - in view of the low surface and underwater speed of the submarine -an overhauling manoeuvre in daylight is bound to succeed depends on the speed of the enemy and his position when sighted. If the enemy escort is well forward of the ships, or if the enemy has an air escort, so that the submarine is forced to dive both frequently and prematurely, thus further reducing its already low speed, the overhauling manoeuvre meets with an additional serious difficulty. But in this one case also, the submarine commander must show determination, and not yield anything unnecessarily.

118 - If the submarine is temporarily forced under the surface by the enemy escort, etc., it must not stay down too long. It should always try to surface again as soon as possible, in order to observe the enemy better and not to lose valuable time without a good reason.

119 - In case of sudden deterioration of visibility, due to squalls of rain, etc., caution should be observed. The submarine should

submerge again, if improving visibility reveals that it has approached too near to the enemy while unable to see him.

120 - When the submarine has reached the necessary position forward of the enemy's beam, that is to say, the counter D/F position in relation to the general course ascertained for the enemy (see No. 108), it must move toward the enemy on the surface and underwater, always in the endeavour to get in a shot (discharge a torpedo) as soon as possible, before the position changes, i.e., before, for example, the enemy changes course, in such a way as to foil the attack.

121 - Free
122 - Free
123 - Free
124 - Free

c) Carrying Out the Underwater Attack

125 - The "sparing" use of the periscope (see Section I, B, No. 31); i.e., the raising of the periscope, at frequent intervals and for a brief space of time, to surface level, so that the periscope appears no bigger than a fist, and is almost constantly awash, begins at a distance of approximately 4,000-5,000m from the enemy, according to the state of the weather and the conditions of light. It is a mistake to keep the periscope down for any length of time when the enemy is near. In that case the submarine is not less visible than during the "sparing" use of the periscope; but it can itself see nothing, and is therefore in greater danger. Consequently, the submarine should carry out frequent observations of short duration; but, in all circumstances, they should be repeated again and again.

126 - The periscope should only be raised when the submarine is travelling at low speed. Before raising the periscope, it is therefore necessary to reduce the speed. Otherwise, if the sea is calm, the wake of the periscope can easily be seen, besides which the periscope of a submarine travelling at speed will cause splashes, and a conspicuous feather ("Wasserfahne").

127 - If special reasons require that the speed be temporarily increased, for example, in order to reach a position more suitable for launching an attack, the periscope must be lowered until the top of it is at least 1m under the surface. When the submarine is at the depth for attack, the periscope should not, however, be further lowered to an extent greater than it is absolutely necessary, in order not unnecessarily to lose time in raising it again.

128 - In a calm sea, the screw of the submarine causes a slight ripple which is visible on the surface. If it is necessary in this case to proceed at speed, the periscope should therefore be taken down altogether, and the submarine should dive to 18m, insofar as the position (nearness) of the enemy will allow this.

129 - Towards the end of the attack, just before the torpedo is launched, it must suffice for the torpedo aimer ("T.C.O."), on completing the computation of the enemy's course and position, to see only the tops of the funnels and masts of the enemy.

130 - For computing the range, the 1 magnification should be used in the periscope. With the 6-fold magnification, no estimation of distance is Possible, on account of the monocular optical system of the periscope.

As a matter of principle, the 6-fold magnification of the periscope should always only be used temporarily, in order the better to observe details of the enemy ship, as, for example, in computing its course and speed, but never for the actual attack at dose range.

131 - At a distance of about 4,000 to 2,000m, according to the speed and position of the enemy, the submarine begins to go in for the attack.

The following rule of thumb serves to determine, in good time, the distance of the submarine when about to launch the attack (torpedo) abreast of the enemy:

In position 5°, the lateral distance from the enemy = $^1/_{10}$, in position 10° = $^1/_5$, in position 15° = $^1/_4$, in position 20° = $^1/_3$, in position 30° = $^1/_2$, of the momentary distance.

132 - The danger of being located by sound location during the attack at dose range must be countered, as far as circumstances allow, by travelling at as slow a speed as possible, and by absolute silence on board the submarine (see Section I, B, II and III).

133 - The underwater attack is also practicable at dawn and dusk, and on moonlit nights. In these cases, the following points should be observed:

    a. Complete blacking out of the conning tower and the control room is necessary, as otherwise the light is still reflected, to a considerable extent, in the periscope.

    b. The estimation of distances and positions at night by means of the periscope meets with great difficulties. The submarine may easily be nearer to the enemy than is supposed.

    c. At night, all periscope operations should be undertaken with the 1 magnification, on account of the improved effect of the optical system when using small magnifications.

It is quiet in the diesel room when moving underwater. The engine watch has time to pick up the magazines they have read so often. Was something missed last time? Otherwise it will soon be time for the popular novels that are available by the crate load.

d. The observation of the enemy against whom the attack is directed, and the all-round view in respect of the position in relation to other nearby vessels, can then be undertaken, in certain circumstances, by two periscopes.

134 - The rare opportunity of attacking an enemy concentration of ships must be used, by going all out, with all the torpedoes,

The commander, already wearing his waterproofs, waits in the control room, in order to be the first to jump up to the bridge. He has just ordered: "Go to periscope depth". When it is up, he will be able to observe the situation outside through the periscope and then give his orders. At the front, the control room petty officer writes down every engine and rudder order with the time so that later, the navigator can calculate the course covered and "connect the cutlery". In front of the chief engineer is the control room seaman who is ready to make his report on the state of the engines, to the commander. (Taken during a pursuit with a U-Boat trap).

even in spite of the strongest enemy escort. One of the ships of the concentration should be attacked, and the attack carried out, by a method suited to the position of the target, in a manner calculated to annihilate the latter; immediately afterwards a second and third ships should be attacked where possible.

135 - The shape of a concentration of ships is difficult to make out from periscope depth, and at a distance. If the enemy group is a broad one (blunt formation, line abreast, double line ahead, broken formation) it is advantageous to let one's self run into the formation from the front, and to fire torpedoes from an angle. The advantages of this position in the enemy group are: less efficient covering and less vigilance on the part of the enemy, and consequently maximum deliberation in carrying out the attack.

In attacking a pointed formation, the open side is more favourable, because the chances of a hit are better (the targets overlap). In addition, on the open side the submarine is in less danger of being rammed, and can therefore carry out the attack with more deliberation.

136 - If, during an attack on a convoy, the necessity arises of diving suddenly to a depth of 20m, as a protection against escorting ships or air attack (i.e., because there is a danger of being rammed or spotted) the attack must on no account be finally abandoned because of that necessity. In view of the fact that, when travelling at the depth of 20m, the submarine loses count of the position in the direction of the attack, it may then in certain circumstances be advisable to turn away from the convoy, at full speed, and to turn down again with little divergence from the general course of the enemy, in order to resume the attack from the outside. If the convoy is a long one, there is then always a chance of getting in a shot at the last ships.

137 - Free

138 - Free

139 - Free

140 - Free

d) Methods of Attack;
Underwater Discharging of Torpedoes

141 - The ordinary underwater attack is carried out with the aid of the fire control system, at maximum range. If the entire fire control system fails to function, and in the case of unexplained misses, the bow torpedo attack proper is called for. These methods of attack must also be mastered by the submarine commander, and used according to circumstances.

i) Maximum Range Attack

142 - Advantages of the maximum range attack:

    a. The commander is free from the necessity of calculating the direction of the attack, and of manoeuvring on this course, and can devote his attention entirely to securing a favourable position for the attack. The only necessity is to get the target into the angle covered by the torpedoes with the minimum firing range.

    b. The possibilities of using the torpedo are considerably greater, as in case of necessity, the entire angle range of the torpedo can always be exploited, and the torpedo discharged in any direction.

    c. The fire control system takes into account the parallax in the torpedo tube, so that, if the firing data are correct, the marking point usually coincides with the centre of the target.

    d. The range can always be read off, and the angle of dispersion (transfer) and the turning circle of the

During the trip underwater, the radio petty officer, sitting in his booth, checks the area around the boat for sounds. He sits in front of his listening device with his earphones on, all ears. He lets it slowly wander across all directions.

submarine can quickly be embodied in the calculation for improving the aiming angle, and used through the medium of the fire control system.

e. Difficult and quickly changing situations (high speed of the enemy, frequent changes of course) can be mastered by a submarine with fire control in circumstances in which a submarine without fire control is forced to renounce the torpedo attack because of the inability of the submarine to turn quickly under water.

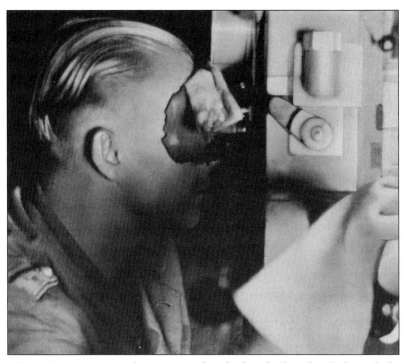

"Raise Periscope!" At the moment when he lets the lens break through the water surface, (if it went up too slowly and too far, the enemy would see it, rapidly leave the area and aim the weapons at the attacking boat) the commander has to check his calculations, order corrections to the torpedo settings, and fire, i.e., release the torpedo. He needs thorough training and experience, unbelievable concentration and quick powers of comprehension, but also a quite specific imagination in order to fire a torpedo accurately. And to be successful, he definitely also has to be integrated into a team with the chief engineer and the entire technical crew.

143 - The important difficulty of the maximum range torpedo attack and this also applies to every angle attack - is the accurate computation of the distance as a basis for the improvement of the convergence. In case of uncertainty in assessing the distance, more especially in firing at dose range, and during engagements *en passant*, one should therefore always endeavour to fire at as small an angle as possible, in order to avoid missing as a result of false convergence values. If the angle is large, a false calculation of distance, especially of distances under 1,000m, results in materially wrong measurements on the target, due to the error of convergence.

144 - In view of the fact that the maximum range attack, when carried out underwater, unlike the bow attack proper, requires complicated technical equipment with a comparatively large personnel, so that the number of possible sources of error is correspondingly greater, careful training of all the operators, and dose attention to the equipment, are a special necessity.

145 - If the electric system of the fire control is out of action do not at once fall back on the primitive methods of the bow, stern or angle attack, but use to the full the reserve possibilities of the plant (predictor as a mechanical firing angle computer). There should be frequent rehearsals of the procedure to be applied when the electric system of the fire control is out of action.

ii) Bow Torpedo Attack Proper
146 - Procedure:
    a. Determine the enemy's course by position and bearing.
    b. Compute the enemy's speed.
    c. Ascertain the director angle for the required firing position.
    d. Put the submarine on the course for the attack; The

course for the attack = cross D/F of the enemy + (starboard) - (port) director angle, according to whether the starboard or the port of the enemy is to be attacked. If it is intended to attack from a narrower angle, the bearing in the position to be taken up when discharging the torpedo should be set for calculating the course for the attack, instead of the diagonal bearing of the target.

e. By "flanking" the course (i.e., keeping ahead of, or behind, the direction of the attack), the submarine should approach to within close range, and take up a favourable position (near position 90° etc.). In doing this, constant observation of the growth of the enemy's bearing and constantly repeated computations of the distance, while using the periscope sparingly, are a necessity.

f. If the enemy's course has been correctly ascertained, and his speed correctly assessed, the enemy must be in position 90° etc. when he enters the D3A. If this does not happen, the moment of firing must be anticipated or retarded, by discharging the torpedo while turning toward, or away from, the target, in order to exploit a more favourable enemy position.

iii) The Stern Torpedo Attack Proper

147 - The stern torpedo attack proper can only be carried out either when the position of the submarine is to the right, ahead of the enemy, or when, in consequence of a sudden change of course on the part of the enemy, the use of the stern torpedo tube is more advantageous than the use of the bow torpedo tubes.

Procedure:

a. If the submarine is ahead of the enemy, it must go to meet him, in order to carry out the stern torpedo attack.

This is how the enemy is seen through the periscope – and in his natural colours! He is mostly covered by the groundswell of the Atlantic – even if the sea is calm and the distance to the booty is very short. In that case, it is necessary to sense, and cleverly exploit the most favourable moment for observation. One must not be prematurely discovered or all of the effort will have been wasted. The torpedo, with its relatively low speed and range, cannot be fired from too great a distance if it is to strike the victim, which continues to sail and perhaps even change course during the torpedo's running period.

Moving toward the enemy is better than moving with him, because, in this case, the submarine, in turning away to take up the direction of attack, has less turning to do to the extent of the double the D.A. (director angle).

b. Ascertain the course and speed of the enemy.

c. Determine the director angle for the required firing position = 90° etc.

d. Set the submarine on the course for the attack. The change of course should be effected according to the speed at which the enemy is approaching. Do not turn too quickly, as otherwise the range becomes too long. Keep your head. Direction of attack = Counter D/F to cross D/F + (starboard) - (port). According to whether the starboard or the port side is being attacked. If the attack is to take place from a narrower angle, the counter D/F of the D/F in each position envisaged for the discharging of the torpedo, for example, 60°, should be set instead of the counter D/F of the cross D/F of the enemy.

iv) Angled Attack (Gyro Angling)

148 - The angled attack has the following important advantages:

a. The submarine is able to move more freely in carrying out the attack, and need not, as it has to do when making a bow attack proper, approach the enemy almost "end on," keeping the enemy's position, and the distance, under constant observation.

b. The submarine does not cross the courses of the enemy's escorting ships to the same extent as when carrying out the bow torpedo attack proper.

c. In case of a too-closely developed bow attack, or of sudden changes of course on the part of the enemy, it is still possible to fire a torpedo.

d. If the enemy formation is a broad one, the angled attack affords the best opportunity of attacking several targets on either side, by allowing one's self to be overtaken by the formation.

149 - The angled attack consists mainly of: i) The 45° angled shot; ii) The 90° angled shot.

The commander can make use of other methods of angled attack, if he is able to make the necessary calculations during the attack, without their having been especially rehearsed, as have the two most usual methods of angled attack.

i) The 45° angled shot.

150 - Method of carrying out the attack:

    a. Set the submarine on the course:

        i. Bows 45°, angle shot; Running Fight (Bows of the submarine in the same direction as the course of the enemy). Direction of attack (course) = Diagonal D/F of the enemy + (starboard) - (port) (45° + director angle), according to whether the starboard or the port side of the target is to be attacked. When firing from a narrower position, the procedure as in the bow torpedo attack proper, is to set the D/F in the position for launching the torpedo, for the purpose of calculating the direction of attack, for example 60° instead of the diagonal D/F of the target. Engagement *en passant* (bows of the submarine in the opposite direction to the course of the enemy): Direction of Attack (course) = Diagonal D/F of the enemy - (starboard) + (port) (45° - director angle), according to whether the starboard or the port side of the target is being attacked.

ii. 45° stern angled shot:

- Running fight (bows of the submarine in the same direction as the course of the enemy): Direction of Attack = Counter D/F to diagonal D/F of the enemy + (port) (45° = director angle), - (starboard). According to whether the starboard or the port side is attacked. For narrower positions, the procedure in calculating the course (direction of the attack) is the same as has been described in dealing with the other methods of attack, previously mentioned. Engagement *en passant* (bows of the submarine in the opposite direction to the course of the enemy):Direction of Attack (course) = Counter D/F to diagonal D/F of the enemy + (starboard) (45° = director angle), - (port), according to whether the starboard or the port side is attacked.

- Set the director angle. Turn the graduated dial on the rim of the periscope by 45° away from the 0° mark toward the target, and then adjust the director angle from the 45° mark to the position of the target; i.e., if the enemy course is to the left, the director angle must be set to the left of the 45° mark, and vice versa. Points to be observed: The director angle always lies outside the 45° torpedo angle, when the torpedo, before it turns, travels in the same direction as the target (for the bow angle attack in running fights, for the stern angle attack in engagements *en passant*; the director angle lies inside the 45° torpedo angle, when the torpedo, before turning, travels in the opposite direction to the target (for the bow angle attack in engagement *en passant*,

72

He has hit it! A mighty detonation makes the surrounding sea shudder, so that even in a submerged boat running blind, there is absolutely no doubt. A massive column of fire, smoke and water, mixed with bits of the ship, rises hugely upwards, spreads out like a vast, often flaming, mushroom stalk, and after a brief hesitation, collapses in on itself again. The smoke continues to rise, spreading itself out and grasping around with flames and heavy blackness. The hull of the enemy ship is torn, from the pressure of water, so that often the ship's boiler will explode and cause more devastation. On top of that a fire often breaks out.

for the stern angle attack in running fights). In both cases, however, the director angle should always be set in the direction of the target from the 45° mark.

- For convergence 50, allow for forward or backward movement· for the former, when the torpedo, before turning, moves in the opposite direction to the target (for the bow angle attack in engagements *en passant*, for the stern angle attack in running fights), and for the latter, when the torpedo, before turning, moves in the same direction as the target (for the bow angle attack in running fights, for the stern angle attack in engagements *en passant*).

ii) The 90° angled shot

151 - The 90° angled attack should only be used for small convergences; i.e., when the torpedo, before turning, moves in the same direction as the target. It is very difficult to estimate

This heavy tanker has been torn in two, through torpedo strikes and the ensuing oil fire.

the D.A. for large convergences, especially in attacking at short range.

Consequently, the 90° angled shot with a small convergent displacement of the target is used: in running fights in the form of the bow torpedo attack; in engagements *en passant* in the form of the stern torpedo attack.

152 - Procedure.

    a. Set the submarine on the direction of attack (course).

        i. 90° bow angled shot in running fights: Direction of attack (course) = Counter D/F of diagonal D/F - (starboard) + (port) (90° + director angle), according to whether the starboard or port side of the target is being attacked. When attacking from a narrower position, the direction of attack (course) is calculated in the same way as in the methods of attack previously indicated; i.e., instead of the diagonal D/F of the target, the D/F in the position for launching the torpedo, for example 60°, or the counter D/F of the bearing, is used for the calculation.

        ii. 90° stern angled shot in engagements *en passant:* Direction of attack (course) = Diagonal D/F of the target - (starboard) +(port) (90° -director angle), according to whether the starboard or port side of the target is attacked.

    b. Set the director angle. Turn the graduated dial on the rim of the periscope by 90° away from the 0° mark towards the target, and then adjust the director angle from the 90° mark to the position of the target; i.e., if the enemy course is to the left, the director angle must be set to the left of the 90° mark, and vice versa (see also No. 146, b).

c. For the convergence allow room for backward movement.

153 - The chief difficulty of the maximum range torpedo attack -and this also applies to every angled attack - is the precise calculation of the distance as a basis for the improvement of the convergence. In case of uncertainty in estimating the distance (range), more especially in launching torpedoes at close range, and during engagements *en passant*, the object to be achieved is always to fire at the minimum angle, in order to avoid misses resulting from false convergence values. If the angle is large, a false estimation of distance, especially of distances under 1,000m, results in materially wrong measurements on the target, due to the error of convergence.

154 - Free
155 - Free
156 - Free
157 - Free
158 - Free
159 - Free
160 - Free
161 - Free
162 - Free
163 - Free
164 - Free
165 - Free
166 - Free
167 - Free
168 - Free
169 - Free
170 - Free

e) Use (Expenditure) of Torpedoes

171 - As far as the supply of torpedoes allows, several shots, in the form of multiple discharges (double or three-fold discharges) should be directed against worthwhile targets, even at short range, and when the data (calculations) are not in doubt. In this case, all the torpedoes should hit the mark, in order to ensure the annihilation of the enemy. This means that the torpedoes should be fired at different parts of the target.

172 - If the range is over 1,000m, or if there is uncertainty as regards the aiming data (high speed of the enemy, several torpedoes (2, 3, or 4) should be released on the "fan" pattern. The idea is to make sure of one hit. It is better to score only one hit than to miss the target with each of several consecutive shots.

Wreckage floats uselessly and abandoned in the long sea-swells, and has to be sunk individually, otherwise it could happen that the Brits find the remains, tow them away and rebuild. That is cheaper, easier and quicker than any new construction.

The target should therefore be covered by aiming at the boundaries of the area of dispersion on the target; i.e., the shots should be spread by the width of the dispersion area in relation to one shot aimed on the basis of the estimated data (if 2 or 4 shots are fired, in relation to an imaginary middle shot).

If a final shot is necessary to sink the damaged ship, remember that the number of misses at the kill is proportionally greater than in firing during the attack.

a. At the kill, steer the submarine ahead of the stationary target, in position 90° at range 2,000 to 3,000m, and approach slowly, carefully keeping the course, to find out whether the enemy is still making headway. When the alteration of steering has been measured, the speed of the target should be set on the director angle computer, or the enemy should be finished off by the bow or stern torpedo attack proper. The speed of the enemy should be taken into account in determining the displacement of the marking point on the target.

b. Go in as close as possible, range under 1,000m. On moonlit nights and during the daytime, submerge once more and attack underwater at 400 to 500m.

c. If, in remote sea areas, an early arrival of enemy defence forces is not to be anticipated, the final shot should not be precipitated. Many ships sink only after 2 to 3 hours.

d. If enemy anti-submarine forces are sighted (naval or air), the final torpedo should be fired at once.

e. In the circumstances described under C, it should be ascertained whether the target can be destroyed by gunfire, instead of by the final torpedo. See also No. 277.

174 - Free

f) What to do After the Underwater Attack

175 - If at all possible, the submarine should remain at periscope depth, in order to carry out observations after the underwater attack, and of deciding whether another torpedo is needed to complete the destruction of the enemy.

Motto: "Better to destroy little than to damage much!"

176 - Exploit the position for attack taken up near the convoy, or in the vicinity of several objectives, for the purpose of discharging several torpedoes in quick succession at several targets, making use of the possibilities of the fire control system. It is not certain that so favourable a position for attack will again be attained. See No. 171.

177 - If the submarine remains at periscope depth after the attack, it will have the advantage of being able to observe the methods and extent of the enemy counteraction, besides finding fresh opportunities of attack. In this way the submarine is also enabled to discover gaps in the pursuing forces of the enemy, through which it can escape.

178 - If there is no further possibility of attack, the submarine should leave the scene of action. If there is a danger of pursuit by sound location the submarine should then travel at "sound location speed."

If there is no danger of being discovered by sound location, on account of interference resulting from sounds proceeding from the enemy, the submarine should leave the scene of action, and get out of the direction of the torpedo, at full speed.

179 - Do not go deep down unless it is absolutely necessary. If you do so you render yourself blind and helpless. Consequently,

do not dive to low depths unless the danger threatening from enemy covering ships in the immediate neighbourhood, is real and imminent.

180 - If the submarine is forced to dive after the underwater attack, on account of the dangerous proximity of enemy hunting units, then it should first go down at full speed in a direction leading away from the scene of action and the direction of the torpedo. During the first confusion on the surface after a torpedo hit, or during the dropping of depth charges, the enemy escort will operate neither with ASDIC nor with sound location. Do not resume the reconnaissance patrol until you have put some distance, horizontally and vertically, between the submarine and the scene of action, where the submarine was sighted by the enemy.

A freighter – open, loaded with heavy war materials – has been buckled in the middle by a torpedo strike. It floats on for a while because the air in the bow and stern cannot escape so quickly and buoys up the wreck. The gun with which British merchant ships are armed - contrary to international custom - can be seen on deck. For this reason they are not merchant, but war ships. Freighters with a floating cargo (e.g., wool, wood etc.) don't like to sink. Iron ore and war materials go down happily.

After the boat has dived, and the steering gear has been adapted to the required depth, put everything out of action, listen carefully, in order to find out what the enemy is doing, and act accordingly.

181 - Always go down dynamically to a low depth! Flooding is a mistake: The submarine automatically becomes heavier with increasing depth (leaking of the stern stuffing boxes and other openings, reduction of volume (contraction) of the body of the submarine) and it may well happen that it drops to a greater depth than is intended. Consequently in diving to considerable depths, the maximum engine power should be used, and it is even advisable to pump out the boat (for example, in the case of Type VII, approximately 1 ton).

182 - In steering the submarine downward to reach the required low depth, the trimming should at first be carried out by boat-hands, if it transpires that the hydroplanes are temporarily not sufficient; trimming with water is not a necessity until the submarine has reached the required depth, and is being steered into it. Care should be exercised in trimming by boat-hands; "all-hands" manoeuvres should not be called for unnecessarily but only in dangerous situations.

183 - Do not go down to an unnecessary depth, as this may also be dangerous: the stern stuffing boxes and other fastenings leak badly, the joints are subject to heavy strain. Always choose the lesser danger, by weighing up the danger from depth charges against the danger of an increased (pressure) eruption of water.

184 - Concerning the measures to be taken against pursuit by ASDIC and position finding, see Section IV.

185 - Return to periscope depth only after careful investigation of sound location and ASDIC (operations of the enemy).

186 - When the submarine is being brought up from a great depth, all the fastenings should be gradually loosened, especially if any of them have been tightened in order to adapt the boat to the depth conditions.

187 - Before surfacing after cruising at a great depth, the steering gear should first be adapted to periscope depth, so as to be able to dive again at once after surfacing, in case of an alarm.
188 - Before surfacing, reduce as far as possible any excessive air pressure in the submarine, by means of the pump.

189 - After surfacing, before emptying the compressed air cells, the surface of the sea should be carefully but quickly examined from the conning tower (see also Section I, B, No. 29)

190 - Free
191 - Free
192 - Free
193 - Free
194 - Free

THE SURFACE TORPEDO ATTACK

a) Fundamental Rules for the Night Surface Attack

195 - The surface torpedo attack by the submarine can only be carried out at night. The object of the surface attack is the same as that of the underwater attack, and dependent on the same ballistic factors; i.e., the torpedo attack at short range which is carried out without warning and takes the enemy by surprise (see Section II, A, No. 91).

196 - Conditions affecting the night attack vary considerably. They depend on the sort of enemy one has to deal with, on the enemy escort, on the course and speed of the enemy, on the conditions of visibility and light, the state of the sea, etc. The torpedo will therefore be discharged from many different positions, and varying distances, depending on the various speeds and changing course of the submarine, according to whether it is travelling on a straight course, or turning sharply, at the same time evading the enemy cover. Because of the low speed of the submarine, the commander will therefore, as a general rule, be under the necessity of attacking from the position which offers itself, at the time of encountering the enemy.

197 - There are, therefore, no hard and fast rules for the surface night attack. It is only possible to establish the following fundamental rules as generally correct:
  a. Analogously to the torpedo-boat attack, the night surface attack by the submarine should be launched,

whenever possible, from a position forward of the beam, of 60° to 90°.

b. The course of the surface attack should always be run by compass, as the submarine commander is otherwise liable to lose count of the position.

c. In the overhauling manoeuvre, constant use must be made of off, and the movement of the enemy D/F must be constantly observed. The attack must not be given up, even when the bearing only moves slowly. If, in spite of every effort, the attack cannot be carried out in daylight, it must be successfully made during the night. These values are almost always more exact than

The point of sinking is marked only by wreckage coming up; often oil and soot from burnt fuel that floats on the surface, as well. Soon, wind and sea swells will drive them apart over "the seven seas of the world". The shipwrecked crews often row towards the distant shore in very unseaworthy, neglected lifeboats; many seamen who sailed for England float around on bits of wreckage. The German boat will often help them if its own safety is not compromised. The English often abandon their people if German U-Boats are operating in the vicinity.

the values estimated during the attack. Assessment by night (i.e., of distances, positions, etc.) is a question of long experience, and requires much practice.

d. At night, important miscalculations may easily occur in the firing data (range finding, etc.). At night, the submarine should therefore go in as close as possible so that even serious miscalculations cannot take effect to any great extent, on account of the short course of the torpedo. Even if the submarine should be sighted during the attack, it must no longer be possible for the enemy to avoid the torpedo.

e. The minimum range for the night attack is also 300m (see Section II, A, No. 92).

f. At night, the discharging of the torpedo should not take place prematurely from too small an angle on the bow. Inexperienced torpedo-aimers (T.C.O.) have the tendency to regard the angle on the bow, at night, as smaller than it really is. The submarine commander should therefore keep his head, and not give a premature firing signal.

g. A certain indication of the speed of the enemy is provided by the extent of the turning manoeuvres in following him - dependent on the distance - on a straight course.

h. Distances are already underestimated at night (see Section 11, A, No. 99). Do not let yourself be misled by the increasing size of the shadow of the target, and fire too early at too long a range.

198 - During the night surface attack, the submarine can:
   a. Be sighted,
   b. Be sound-located,
   c. Be located by ASDIC.

i) Danger of Being Sighted

199 - As a matter of principle, the submarine commander should bear in mind that the submarine is always more difficult to see at night than any surface ship, unless the conditions of light are exceptionally unfavourable. The reliance of the commander on the invisibility of his boat at night will increase with each new experience. Every contrary feeling must be overcome by the consideration that the enemy whom the submarine is attacking, being on the defensive, is in a weaker position, more especially as his lookout, in consequence of long and gruelling periods of duty, is in no position to keep as good a watch as the submarine, which, at the moment, is concentrating all its energy and attention on the development of the attack.

200 - The difficulty of detecting the submarine at night on the surface is due to its long and low silhouette, since it disappears almost entirely in the water, even including the conning tower. The conning tower can be most easily detected by the enemy when it rises above the dip of the horizon, from the line of sight of the enemy. This is the danger zone for the approaching submarine. Against the background of the sea alone, the conning tower is very difficult to make out.

201 - The conning tower of the submarine always appears as a darker object, both in the dip of the horizon and against the background of the sea, and even on the darkest night. In our latitudes, the most suitable colour for the conning tower, according to the experiences gained, is a light grey or a dull white-grey; in the Atlantic, a dark blue-grey.

202 - In view of the fact that paint, especially on the wet submarine, is liable to reflect the light (shine), care must be taken

not to show the enemy the moon-lit side. If the circumstances make this unavoidable, the tapering silhouette should be turned toward him as soon as possible.

203 - Take care that the submarine does not appear in the track of the moon on the water; i.e., in the line between the moon and the target.

204 - Favourable conditions of attack, enabling the submarine to remain:
  a. Attack the enemy when he can be seen against the light horizon, or against the moon, and move toward him from the direction of the dark horizon, or the dark portion of the sea. In this case, the submarine itself is invisible even at the shortest distances from the enemy.

The boat floats, rising up and down for weeks, surrounded by loneliness in the area it was assigned to. Possibly, the hunt for a freighter was in vain. For days, nothing has been seen in the Atlantic. Where does it end? Where does it begin? Nothing but the immeasurable, surrounding space, cradled by the wind and wandering swells, the clouds, sunshine and rain, weather and storms changing unpredictably by day and night. And the German flag on the mast.

b. Go in with the sea, from windward, in order to reduce the head sea, which may well attract attention, especially if the sea is calm. For the same reason it is advisable to proceed at low speed when close to the enemy. This will also have the effect of reducing the stern sea, which is apt to betray the submarine if the water is smooth. In addition, the windward side has the advantage that it renders observation more difficult for the enemy, more particularly in a strong wind, or during rain.

c. During the attack it is always necessary and correct, to approach the enemy, up to the point of discharging the torpedo; i.e., of turning to fire the torpedo, in such a way as to show him the narrow outline of the submarine. The head sea and the stern sea then merge into one, and the

As the twilight sinks, the boat reaches the open sea of northern Biscay. The bridge is still occupied by the off-duty men, apart from the lookout. They enjoy the fresh air for the last time. The coast sinks away in the distance. The evening rises up, the first night of the long-range operation. The mission against the enemy has begun.

form of the body of the boat itself, which might betray itself by contours of foam if it presented a larger surface to the enemy, is then sure to be invisible. A favourable method of attack is therefore to keep the submarine in the narrow position, and keep on turning, to show only the narrow outline of the submarine the approach by the "dog course" ("Hundekurve").

d. Caution should be observed during the transition from night to day, on account of the rapid alteration of the range of vision.

205 - Free

206 - Free

ii) Danger of Being Sound-Located

207 - The sound of the submarine's engines is for practical purposes inaudible on the surface, through the air, more especially in view of the sounds proceeding from the enemy.

208 - To what extent the other sounds made by the submarine when travelling on the surface (noise of the screws, etc.) can be sound-located by the enemy, and distinguished as submarine noises from the sounds made by the enemy himself, which increase in proportion to his speed and the Condition of the sea, depends on the circumstances dealt with in Section I, 8, II.

If the conditions for sound-locating are good, a submarine propelled by diesel engines and travelling on the surface can, however, be heard much more distinctly than a submarine with electric motors travelling underwater or on the surface. If, therefore, enemy sound location is to be anticipated and especially if the speed of the enemy is slow and the sea calm, the attempt must be made to go in for the attack on electric motors provided that the position of the submarine in relation to the enemy will allow this considering the slow speed of the electric motors.

209 - Free

210 - In no circumstances should the danger of enemy sound location during the night attack be overestimated, and the opportunity of carrying out a fatal attack at short range be neglected on that account (see Section II A, No. 94)

211 - Free
212 - Free
213 - Free

The bridge watch keeps going in heavy waterproofs. It is a long time to keep lookout for the enemy, wet and damp and exhausted from the rolling sea swells and whipped by the wind and hail. Nonetheless, isn't it wonderful to be alive, to assert yourself against nature storming in.

iii) Danger of Being Located by ASDIC

214 - It will only be in rare cases, when the sea is calm and the enemy speed slow, that a submarine on the surface is located by ASDIC. The conditions governing the hunting operations to be directed against a submarine on the surface are usually less favourable than when the ASDIC is applied to a submarine cruising underwater in a quiet area, on account of the higher interference level on the surface (constant permeation of the surface of the water with air by the movement of the sea and the vessel).

215 - The danger from enemy submarine detecting operations (ASDIC) should consequently be no more overestimated than the danger of being sound-located, and should on no account lead to the abandonment of the attack (see Section 11, A, No. 94).

216 - It must be assumed that some warships are provided with surface position finding equipment (surface anti-submarine detecting gear) ("Dete"). The suspicion that this is so must not, however, cause the commander to think that he has been located each time the enemy, or the covering ships of the enemy, appear to execute a special manoeuvre, and thereupon to give up his attack. In almost all such cases, the movements of the enemy are evasive movements which happen to be taking place at the time. It is not until it is quite certain that the enemy movements mean that the submarine is being pursued that the latter should leave the scene of operations and submerge if the enemy comes into sight. Further action according to No. 180. Sudden change of course either before submerging, or when going down. Remember that the first and most dangerous depth charges are dropped on the spot where the submarine has dived, and on the

course which the enemy supposes the submarine will follow in leaving the theatre of operations.

217 - Free
218 - Free

b) Carrying out the Night Surface Attack

219 - The general rules for the use of the submarine for the underwater attack (see Section II, B, No. 105) apply logically also to the night surface attack. Special attention is called to the necessity of obtaining reliable ballistic calculations (firing data) even at night, and in all circumstances and by all possible means (overtaking: see No. 105, e).

220 - In sea areas where contact with the enemy may be expected at night, at least one torpedo must be carried in the tube, with the tube opened ready for action. If the enemy is sighted suddenly, there may in certain circumstances not be enough time to open the tube.

221 - In war, the success or failure of night operations is more than ever dependent on good eyesight and a good lookout. He who sees first always has the advantage. Consequently, the place for the people who can see best at night is the conning tower, more especially during the attack itself.

The lookout should be kept at night with binoculars only. In (heavy) rain, or heavy seas, a man should be sent on to the conning tower for the special purpose of holding dry glasses ready and wiping wet glasses.

222 - When a target is sighted, first show the narrow side, keep the course, ascertain the change in bearing, and try later to

reach a position ahead of the beam, travelling at top speed on the confines of the enemy's range of sight, in order to be able to carry out the attack proper from the forward position. Do not give up the attempt to bring the submarine forward to a position ahead of the beam, and thus to make the attack, even when the excess of speed of the submarine appears only slight. Changes of course on the part of the enemy may alter the chances of success of the submarine at any moment.

223 - The most favourable quarter (dark horizon, windward side, etc.) should already be selected while the submarine is on the way to take up its Position for the attack. If the circumstances are such that the overhauling Process will probably last some time, it will be necessary, on moonlit nights, to take into account the change of the lunar azimuth up to the time of the attack proper.

The men on the bridge are dripping wet. The water fills their high, sea boots to the top. But the boat weathers the storm. The watch only lets out an oath now and again when another wave assaults them. They could submerge after all! Down below it is calm and quiet. But they are not just sailing out to sea! This is war! They are waiting for booty. They are onto the enemy at an advance post! They mustn't miss a thing, not even when the sea is like this.

Torn storm clouds charge along beneath the brightening sky. A huge groundswell has risen up. The comb breaks foaming over their heads. The boat climbs up the slopes with great effort and then glides more swiftly down again. Softly, adapting, the boat leaves its course, whilst the blind giants beneath it continue to rage as though they take no notice of it. These small German boats have wonderful nautical characteristics. They are carried comfortingly, like living creatures. The larger the ship, the stiffer and more inorganically it moves through the swells.

If the conditions of light have changed, for any reason, during the overtaking manoeuvre (parting of the cloud cover, etc.), it may be necessary to manoeuvre round to the other side for the purpose of carrying out the attack.

224 - Free
225 - Free
226 - Free

c) Carrying out the Surface Night Attack

227 - After having reached the desired position ahead of the enemy's beam, the attack proper commences. In this case, the most important rule to be observed is: remain in the narrow position until the torpedo is discharged - keep the "dog's course." Any (even temporary) widening of the outline of the submarine may betray it.

228 - When attacking, keep the submarine underway; otherwise evasive action on the surface, or emergency diving during or after the attack, in face of enemy escorting forces, is not possible in time.

229 - On meeting with enemy escorting ships, try to evade them, as far as is possible, without submerging, in order to retain your mobility, and be able to take in the situation. On the surface, the submarine commander remains master of the situation. If the submarine submerges, it becomes blind and stationary, and must leave it to the enemy to bring about any change of the position on the surface.

230 - The advantage of the narrow outline in attacking is ensured by the fire control system.

231 - On meeting an enemy concentration, advantage must be taken of this rare opportunity, at night as well as in daytime, by utilizing to the full possibilities of the boat and the torpedoes. After the first target, a second and a third target should be attacked at once. The confusion among the enemy forces which usually occurs at night, after the launching of the first torpedo, will make this easier.

232 - As regards multiple shots and "fan shooting," the rules laid down for underwater firing of torpedoes (see Section II, E, Nos. 171 to 174) also apply to the surface use of torpedoes.

233 - Free
234 - Free

d) What to do After the Night Surface Attack

235 - After the night surface attack, the commander should endeavour to stay on the surface, in order to observe the success of the attack, and, if conditions are favourable, to organize a second and third attack. Do not go deep down unless it is necessary; going down renders you blind and helpless. On the surface, the commander continues to be able to take in the situation, and retains his liberty of action. The submarine should, therefore, only submerge when compelled to do so by direct pursuit.

236 - After firing the torpedo, it will in most cases be right to turn at once sharply toward the enemy's stern, in order as quickly as possible to get out of the dangerous sector ahead of the enemy's beam, in which the danger of being sighted and rammed is greatest.

237 - If the submarine is able to remain on the surface after the attack, it should make a short run outward, in order to be able to get in the next torpedo as soon as possible.

238 - If the submarine is forced to dive, on account of the development of the pursuit, then it should first do so at top speed, and proceed in a direction leading away from the scene of action and the course of the torpedo. In doing this, it is unnecessary to take into account any danger of sound location. After a hit at night, there is such confusion on the surface that the enemy anti-submarine detecting service will not be able, with any degree of

Sometimes, the sea just rises, climbs up and over the boat irresistibly, over the tower and the watch on the bridge, who are securely fastened. The lookout even finds time to kick the tower hatch closed, so that the sea doesn't break in and their ship and all in it sink for ever. Mostly however, the giants take it on their backs willingly and release it again like an annoying insect that is hardly noticed. It carries the boat like a floating seagull when the raging mountain passes over. Indignantly, the boat shakes the water from its grey flanks.

certainty, to sound-locate, or locate by ASDIC any submarine travelling below the surface.

239 - The submarine should make off, underwater, at full speed on a straight course, in order to take the shortest way out of the area covered by the enemy defence. It will be able the sooner to surface again.

The direction of retreat should be an oblique forward course in relation to the course of the enemy, not a backward course, so that the submarine may again ground to windward of the enemy, even under water, preparatory to carrying out the next attack.

240 - How far the submarine should move away underwater after the dive depends on the condition of the atmosphere (visibility). The enemy must still be in sight when the submarine surfaces again; but the submarine itself must not be spotted on surfacing. Generally speaking, a run of 2,000 to 3,000m will suffice.

241 - In surfacing, the submarine should observe the rules laid down for that purpose: sound-location, then quickly charge the air pressure tanks, no time to be lost in opening the man hole of the conning tower, all-round view.

Watch the enemy and empty the cells altogether, according to the circumstances.

If another attack is practicable, go forward at once and carry out the attack.

242 - For rules of action in case of underwater pursuit by the enemy, see Section IV, Nos. 246 to 269.

243 - Free

244 - Free

245 - Free

SECTION IV

ACTION TO BE TAKEN IN CASE OF DEFENSIVE ACTION AND PURSUIT BY THE ENEMY

246 - The object of the enemy anti-submarine defence and offensive action is the destruction of the submarine, either by direct armed attack underwater, or by keeping the submarine underwater to the point of exhaustion, and then destroying it when it surfaces.

247 - As a matter of principle, the submarine which is the object of enemy underwater pursuit should behave in such a way that it remains active, and should try to make good its escape by availing itself of every possibility, instead of simply waiting, and lying passively at the bottom. Activity on the part of the submarine always offers the best chances of shaking off the enemy.

248 - In all operations, the chief danger for the submarine is at the beginning, when the enemy, having witnessed the attack by the submarine, and seen it submerge, is best able to assess its position, and the submarine has not yet reached any great depth.

Consequently, if the submarine has been detected, it should leave the scene of the attack, or the spot where it has submerged, at full speed, and go deep down without troubling about the possibility of being sound-located.

249 - Free

When the sea is heavy, the breakers smack against the tower hatch and down into the control room and need to be pumped out. If the sea gets too rough, the hatch is closed. Then the watch on the bridge stands outside, without direct contact to the rest of the boat, alone in the wild ocean; an unforgettable experience.

a) **What to do when pursued by Sound Location**

250 - Attention is called to the general remarks concerning enemy sound location: Section I, B, II, Nos. 46 to 54.

    Suggestions as to the possibilities of shaking off the enemy:

a. Take the D/F sound location of the enemy astern.

b. Eliminate all sources of noise in the submarine: stop all auxiliary machinery which is not indispensable (pumps, ventilators, compressors, periscope motor, gyroscopic compass - above all, the secondary gyroscopes - etc.); main rudder and hydroplane should be operated by hand; pumping out, and trimming, with air; depth steering as far as possible only by head list, and then trimming by hand.

c. Absolute silence of the crew on board the submarine; speaking in low tones, working silently, moving about in stockinged feet, etc.

d. Go down very deep; the deeper the position of the submarine, the greater the probability of being incorrectly sound-located.

e. Run out and double at a good distance, and then make off on a straight course, in order to get well away from the pursuing enemy forces. Do not double frequently, or continually zigzag, because this results in loss of distance.

f. If possible, get away in the wake of the enemy's screw, on account of the effective interference level affecting his reception in sound location.

g. Accelerate your speed when the enemy accelerates (or when depth charges are detonated), and stop, or slow down to minimum r.p.m. of the engine, when the enemy stops.

251 - Free

252 - Free

253 - Free

b) What to do in Case of Pursuit by ASDIC

254 - Attention is called to the general remarks about anti-submarine position finding: Section I, B, III, Nos. 55 to 64.

Measures to be taken against anti-submarine position finding:

a. Show the narrow outline (see No. 59) in order to offer the minimum echo sounding surface.

b. Go low down, and during the dive carry out consecutive measurements of the density and temperature of the water, with a view to ascertaining which stratum of water affords protection against the enemy ASDIC operations -a condition characterized by a weakening of the echo impulses (see No. 56, a and b). The weaker the reception of the echo impulses in the hydrophone of the submarine, the weaker, and therefore the more inaccurate, the echo returning to the enemy's submarine-detecting gear. In certain circumstances, a temporary stationing of the submarine on the bottom of the sea is also likely to be successful as a protective measure against depth position finding operations of the enemy. This course can be particularly effective at great depths, because difference of depth of 6 to 8m are then very hard to determine by means of the anti-submarine detecting gear.

c. Absolute silence of the crew on board the submarine (see No. 59, b, No. 250, band c), on account of the possibility of detecting noises in the submarine through the medium of the enemy's anti-submarine gear.

d. Run out to a good distance, and double - no frequent

The chief helmsman, the boat's navigator, or his mate, take every opportunity to "shoot" the sun or the stars with the sextant, their astronomical "cutlery"; because comparing the position of the stars with the chronometer time, they can determine the boat's position, which is calculated from the course and the engine speed, and can control the "cutlery" that is still connected, during the times they can't see anything.

zigzagging - and then make off on a straight course, in order to gain on the hunting vessels.

e. Accelerate your speed when the enemy accelerates his (or when depth charges are detonated); stop or crawl when the enemy stops. Be cautious as regards continued cruising at speed, since the sound of the screw revolving at high velocity, like all other sounds, can be detected with the antisubmarine gear (see Section I, B, IV, No. 59, B).

f. If possible, make your getaway in the wake of the enemy's screw, because the enemy's reception is impaired ("screened") by the disturbance caused by his own screw.

g. In narrow coastal waters (narrow bays, etc.), it is advisable to go in dose to the coast, so as to stand between the enemy's ASDIC gear and the coast (deflection and multiplication of the echoes - see No. 57, B.

h. At distances under 300m from the pursuing enemy, the ASDIC operations are ineffective, because, owing to the short distance, they give practically no results.

255 - Free
256 - Free
257 - Free

258 - According to the observations of which the results are so far available, it seems that the enemy, in many cases, operates with a combined sound locating and deep-sea echo-sounding device. After the submarine has been reported, spotted, or otherwise detected (course of the torpedo, detonation of the torpedo) the hunters endeavour as far as possible to take an accurate D/F bearing of the submarine, probably by means of sound location equipment - for this purpose the pursuit units of the enemy stop

their engines - in order afterwards to approach the submarine, continually echo sounding with the submarine detecting gear, in the direction of bearing and to locate it by simple deep-sea echo sounding.

259 - Passive behaviour on the part of the submarine, consisting in continually lying on the bottom of the sea, results in a danger that the position of the submarine will be betrayed by leakages from certain parts of the body of the boat (traces of oil). Consequently, stationing oneself on the bottom should be resorted to only as a temporary expedient, as a protection against specific deep-sea echo sounding (see No. 254, B), or when the submarine has already sprung a leak.

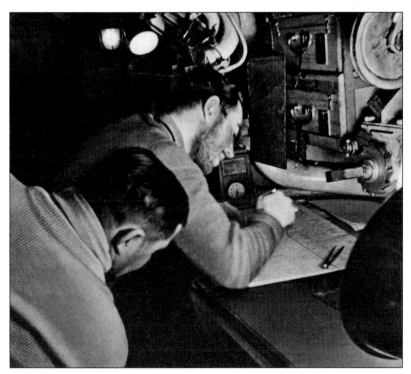

The values that have been noted are reported to the helmsman via the map desk in the control room. He calculates according to the tables, and sets the course on the map using the compass and nautical triangle.

The cook at his work surface in the galley, a board that lies on the waste pipe. The rungs of the stern ladder (which is locked at sea) cut through the middle of the tiny room. Right behind his back is the hot plate, on which the food has to be prepared punctually for over 40 men. On top of that, this room, through which everyone flows to get to the e-engines and diesels, also holds the W.C. There is barely room to fall over in rolling seas!

260 - If attacked with depth charges, keep a close watch on all joints, as these easily become loose as a result of vibrations, making possible large eruptions of water.

261 - If pursued for a long time, the protection afforded by darkness must in all circumstances be used in order to escape. If, in such a case, the darkness has been missed, and if the submarine finds itself, at dawn, still followed and menaced, it may have become too late to escape, especially in seasons and areas with long hours of daylight.

262 - After having travelled for a considerable length of time at great depth, on going up, before surfacing, the following rules should be observed:
   a. all fastenings (joints) to be eased gradually, more especially if they have been tightened on going deep down;
   b. before surfacing, get the steering gear in order again, so as to be ready for an immediate emergency dive after surfacing;
   c. before surfacing, pump off any excess air pressure in the boat.
See also Section II, F, Nos. 185 to 189.

263 - As a matter of principle, every submarine commander - in view of the possibility that he may one day be surrounded by enemy forces and penned in, finding himself in a hopeless position - should plan and prepare the blowing up of the submarine by the crew itself, in every detail, with regard both to the circumstances of such an emergency and the procedure to be followed. Such a possibility must be taken into consideration more especially in the case of enemy operations in shallow water.

264 - Preparatory measures for blowing up your own submarine.

    a. Place blasting charges (petards) for the purpose of creating several big leaks in the body of the boat, in the most suitable positions (bottom valves far admission of cooling water for the diesel engines, bottom valves for admission of sea water for the torpedo bulkheads, diesel fumes exhaust pipe underneath the ceiling with the gas flaps opened).

    b. Place blasting charges (petards) or H.E. cylinders in position for the effective destruction of highly secret equipment (wireless equipment, sound locator and target detecting equipment, periscopes, fire control system, etc.). If there are not enough blasting cartridges and H.E. cylinders available for this purpose, the equipment must be smashed, so that it becomes useless.

    c. Destroy secret documents of special importance by acid treatment; tie the other secret documents in a bundle, especially all wireless code data, and weight the bundles sufficiently with iron parts, for throwing overboard after surfacing.

    d. Expose secret parts and mechanisms of weapons, which, when the submarine is abandoned, must be separately thrown overboard (combat pistols, etc.)

    e. Prepare a brief wireless message, in order to be able to report to Headquarters the destruction by yourself of the submarine, if it should still be possible to surface.

    f. After the submarine has surfaced for the last time, open the diesel head and foot valves, and empty all the compressed air tanks via the discharge valves.

265 - If it becomes necessary to blow up the boat in close proximity to the pursuing enemy, and if the position of the submarine makes it at all possible, the commander should at

this moment still be concerned chiefly with the possibilities of hurting and destroying the enemy, and should use his last weapons to try to fight him.

Then the enemy covering forces should be kept in check with all available means (gun, machine gun, tommy guns, etc.), until all measures for the effective destruction of the submarine have been taken.

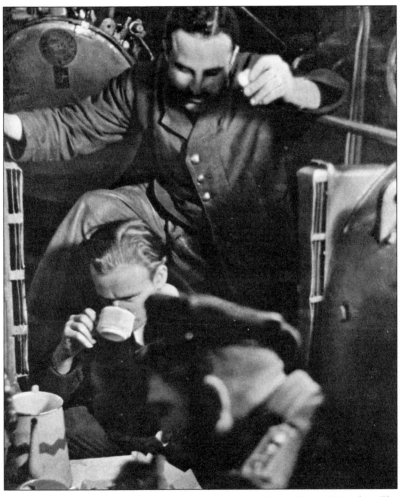

Afternoon coffee hour! An exception, made to celebrate Easter Monday. The chief engineer drinks his on watch at the e-engine in the stern torpedo room. It is a drink with lots of sugar and tinned milk; with biscuits.

c) What to do in Case of Enemy Air Activity

266 - For general rules of action in case of enemy air activity see Nos. 33 to 41.

In areas specially threatened by enemy air activity, the lookout should always be taken by the best members of the crew, the A.A. weapons should be ready for action, and manned, and the serviceability of the weapons should be ensured by frequent replacement and trials (firing tests).

The crew eats and sleeps in the bow. Pepi from eastern Germany, particularly likes the cooked rice. Lütten from the eastern coast prefers tinned ham and Willem from eastern Silesia, who makes sure he gets his share too, ends his evening meal with well-sweetened tea. If the others are not on watch, they have already slid into their bunks right and left. Two of them sit in front of the sleepers; Willem, on the other hand squats on the lemon crate at the head of the unfolded table that does not allow room for everyone. They are moving submerged, otherwise this scene with mountains of empty plates would not be on show.

267 - On passage, the safety of the boat is the chief consideration during operations, the attack. On passage, the submarine should therefore dive as soon as it is known that the enemy planes are trying to locate it (by radar or visual search; when attacking, it should not allow itself to be diverted from its purpose to every reconnaissance operation of enemy planes.

268 - Enemy planes which have located the submarine by radar or visual search, attack, wherever possible, out of the sun, or on the course of the submarine or the direction of diving, and turn on their headlights at night shortly before attacking.

269 - Fundamental rules: When an aircraft that is not flying in the direction of the submarine is sighted in the distance, do not in general submerge, but turn away, show the narrow outline, and reduce speed, so that the line of foam in the wake of the submarine disappears.

If an aircraft sighted in the distance is flying toward the submarine, submerge at once.

If a plane is sighted at night only when its lights go on in flying over, or passing near the submarine, so that it must make another run in order to attack, the submarine should submerge immediately.

If an aircraft flying toward the submarine is sighted so late that the submarine cannot get down in time, do not submerge, but fight off the plane with A.A. weapons. After the first attack, submerge at once, before the plane can make another run.

270 - After submerging during an attack, always go down at once to depth A, and double.

SECTION V
THE SUBMARINE
AS A GUNNERY VESSEL

271 - The submarine as a gunnery vessel is in itself properly a contradiction in terms. Being incapable of offering powerful resistance, and because of its low and unstable gunnery and controlling platforms, which are directly exposed to the action of the sea, it cannot be said to be built for artillery combat. In the use of gunnery, the submarine proper is fundamentally inferior to any surface vessel of war, because every gunnery duel means that for the submarine, unlike its adversary on the surface, everything is at stake, since a hit on the body of the submarine may render it incapable of diving, and thus lead to its total loss. A gunnery duel between the submarine proper, i.e., the torpedo-carrying submarine as a weapon of attack, and surface vessels of war, is therefore impracticable.

272 - For the torpedo-firing submarine, the gunnery is and remains a minor weapon, to be used on occasion, because the use of gunnery openly and on the surface - runs counter to the primary purpose of the submarine, which is the surprise underwater attack.

In accordance with this fundamental fact, the torpedo-firing submarine uses only its gunnery in waging war against merchant shipping, that is to say, for the purpose of stopping steamers, or of overcoming the resistance of unarmed or weakly armed vessels (see Section VII, No. 305).

273 - Every time the commander resorts to the use of gunnery, he must bear in mind that, in wartime, almost all enemy merchant

ships are armed, and that neutral markings are no proof that the ships thus marked really are neutral, and harmless.

274 - The use of gunnery against an armed enemy can only succeed if heavy hits are at once scored on the enemy, at minimum range with the help of the element of surprise, and if the submarine is also in a position to prevent the manning and use of the enemy's gunnery, by bringing all its light weapons to bear on the enemy.

275 -

    a. This achieved by the "gunnery-raid" - at dusk, or after dark, with all weapons at minimum range (6 to 11 km). During the day, or on light moonlit nights, a gunnery attack at long range can only succeed if the enemy is poorly armed, or unarmed.

    b. The preliminary conditions for the success of a gunnery raid are: adequate special training (including night training); careful planning and careful material preparation of the attack; individual training in the use of the individual weapons.

    c. Procedure:

        I. Gun commander and crew take up action stations in good time on the conning tower and the upper deck, in order to get used to the darkness. Precise arrangements are to be made regarding method of covering the target. 10.5cm are to be fired at the bridge and superstructures, beginning with 10 rounds of incendiary shells, in order to get a good marking point in the resulting fire. 3.7cm machine gun m34 to be fired at the stern (gun). 2cm (powerful dazzling effect) should only be fired on orders of the commander, when there is a jam (stoppage) in the 3.7cm gun.

II. After the type and armament of the enemy ship have been ascertained (in case of necessity, by underwater observation during the day):

i. Approach the steamer cautiously from the rear, by stages making use of the conditions of light, sea and wind. Open fire as soon as the submarine is level with the steamer. Range according to darkness, in no circumstances more than 6 to 8km.

ii. or overhaul on the boundary of the zone of visibility to position 50 to 60. Approach on the "dog course," slowly or at full speed, to reach range 800 and position approximately 100. Rudder hard over by 6 to 7 "DEZ" to the direction of the running fight, with a slight shortening of the range. Open fire as soon as you are on the course. This method has the advantage of a quicker passage through the danger zone, and, on the other hand, the disadvantage of attacking from a sector which can be better observed by the enemy.

iii. Or overhaul on the boundary of the zone of visibility until the narrow position is reached, approach on the "dog course," and manoeuvre in such a way that the range in position 90 is about 5 to 8km; then open up with your guns like a bolt out of the blue, at the same time increasing the speed of the submarine. The submarine, firing its guns, passes behind the stern of the enemy ship, and is in a position at any moment to shorten or keep the range, by turning in toward the enemy, or following the course to engage in a running fight, or, if the

Whilst the crew have their own daily rota for a "table man" who fetches the food from the galley, puts it on the table and cleans up, (the potatoes for the entire boat are peeled by everyone in the morning right after waking; all those who are not on watch), the petty officers, and officers have their own "table man" for the length of the trip; he has "do the table", to wash up, open the tins and prepare everything on the plates and in bowls. In the bow, the free life of robbers is fun for the men! In the top bunk on the starboard side, the engine mate is already reading before the green curtain closes in and the light goes out.

enemy puts up a strong defence, to bring about a rapid increase of range by turning away and accelerating its speed.

iv. It is not advisable to fight an engagement *en passant* at the guns fire crosswise, and it is difficult to keep the reckoning, owing to the movement (change of bearing) of the target.

III. The second shot must hit the mark. Bridge and superstructures are big targets, and soon burn. (It is particularly important that the Ships should soon burn, as the gun commanders are dazzled by the

Once again, the small, slim petty officer is the last one sitting at lunch at the partly unfolded table between the bunk partitions in the U-room. There was pea soup with bacon and tinned meat. And a few sausages for everyone. As the others were full up, 16 of them wandered onto his plate. The camera just caught the last one. ("What you peasant, you sneak, did you photograph me?" he jokes, laughing as it clicks). The picture, taken quickly, without lights and unnoticed, documented it after all; Erwin's last three!

flames, and marking is rendered very difficult.) According to circumstances, concentrate the gunfire on one part of the ship. At dose range, machine guns m34 are very effective in suppressing enemy resistance. If, after the first artillery attack, enemy fire is still to be reckoned with, it is advisable to attack with short bursts (approximately 6 to 8 rounds 10.5cm or 8.8cm, and, proportionately, 3.7cm or 2cm), and beat down the enemy resistance without exposing the submarine by staying too long near the enemy. In order to sink the ship quicker the fire should afterwards be directed only at the bows or the stern. On an even keel, ships only sink slowly. Firing from a position ahead of the beam should be avoided, on account of the blinding effect of the flash.

d. In carrying out the artillery raid, a sharp lookout should be kept (first officer of the watch) to leeward of the gunfire. In certain circumstances, it is advisable, as soon as a certain effect of the bombardment is noticed on the enemy ship (collapse of the defence), to interrupt the attack, and to take up a position on the other side of the enemy, in order to watch the sea on that side.

276 - As soon as the enemy ship, in an artillery duel, begins to find the range, the submarine must turn away or submerge.

277 - In areas not frequently patrolled by the enemy, the use of artillery against ships which have been hit by a torpedo, but are still afloat, is likely to be successful, and saves torpedoes. The attack on ships whose engines have been put out of action should be carried out from a position ahead or astern, according to the disposition of the guns.

278 - Hints concerning the use of gunnery.

    a. Before the submarine surfaces for the artillery attack, the gun crew must assemble in the control room ready for action, with all equipment (ammunition cases open, ammunition feed prepared), so as to get the gun ready to fire in the shortest possible time after surfacing.

    b. In carrying out a gunnery attack after surfacing, the order "ready to fire" must not be given until the commander has satisfied himself from the conning tower that the general position, as well as the navigational conditions (submarine sufficiently out of the water) are favourable.

    c. As a matter of principle, the entire gun crew, including those in charge of the magazine, should always be strapped on while working. The danger of falling overboard is great, and the fishing for men who have fallen into water costs valuable time.

    d. Ammunition is to be protected from being wet by splashes (spray). Wet ammunition causes the bursting of cartridge cases, and thereby in certain circumstances troublesome stoppages.

    e. During every gunnery engagement, a constant sharp watch should be kept (air and horizon). Carelessness of the watch is dangerous.

279 - Free

SECTION VI

THE SUBMARINE AS A MINE LAYER

280 - The value of the submarine as a mine layer lies in its use in sea areas dominated by the enemy, which are inaccessible to our own surface forces.

281 - There is not enough room in a submarine to enable it to carry the appropriate number of mines and appliances (means of obstruction) required to construct a barrage calculated to provide the maximum obstruction to enemy minesweeping operations.

Because of the navigational difficulties the laying of barrages by two or more submarines in cooperation, and systematically directed, for the purpose of overcoming these difficulties is not possible in practice, or in the face of enemy counter-operations which may compel one of the submarines to take evasive action of different kinds, or to go deep down.

282 - The pre-conditions for carrying out large-scale, and therefore more effective, mine-laying operations, are far more favourable in the case of the mine-carrying submarine proper. Thanks to the larger number of mines which this type of submarine can carry, it will even be possible for the mine-laying submarine to lay regular mine barrages in narrow entrances (to harbours) etc.

283 - The torpedo submarine, on the other hand, when used for mining operations, is eminently suitable for carrying out contaminations as near as possible to enemy ports, etc. The

more numerous these contaminations in the various suitable stretches of enemy coastal waters, the greater the interference with, and obstruction of, enemy navigation, and the dispersion of the hostile mine-detecting and anti-mine-laying units.

284 - To effect the contaminations, the submarine must stand, before daybreak, as near as possible to the enemy harbour, laying course for it underwater in the first light, and finally, after carefully observing the shipping channels, and taking exact navigational bearings, lay the mines.

The laying of the mines at night on the surface is more difficult on account of the difficult navigational problem of a blacked-out coast, and on account of the danger of being surprised, before the completion of the contamination, by enemy patrol ships, and thus betraying the mining. But war experiences show that, in certain circumstances, mine-laying operations can in fact also be carried out at night, on the surface, and even in spite of a dose enemy watch, if the submarine behaves cleverly enough. 285 - The mines should only be laid close together (minimum spacing = safety interval) when the currents are known, and when the low speed which is usually indispensable in mine-laying can be so well maintained that there is no possibility of the spacing of the mines falling short of the safety minimum. The rope-mine ("TMA") will lend itself rather better to surface laying from the submarine, but the possibilities of reloading are limited by the rolling of the boat due to the motion of the sea.

286 - Free
287 - Free
288 - Free
289 - Free

Towards the end of the mission, in the so-called officers' mess - also just a tiny niche between the high locker walls and the bunks, one of which, belonging to the C.E., serves as a sofa in the daytime - sits the first officer of the watch and writes the log. Here too the whole of life floods through the room because each one is also a corridor in the narrow tube. The C.E. waits beside him on a folding chair for his bunk to become available. In the meantime, he sucks on his beloved lemon with sugar. Because of the tinned food, lemons are indispensable. Most men drink it in tea, some men eat them out of their hands.

SECTION VII

SUBMARINE WARFARE ON MERCHANT SHIPPING

a) General

290 - In the struggle against the enemy sea communications, i.e., in the destruction of the enemy's overseas trade, the submarine is a particularly suitable naval weapon with which to challenge the enemy's naval superiority. The continuous successful use of the submarine in the war on merchant shipping is, therefore, in the long run, of decisive strategical importance for the total course of the war, since the enemy, who is dependent on his overseas trade, is in the position that, for him, the loss of his sea communications means the loss of the war.

291 - The suitability of the submarine for use in the war on merchant shipping depends, again, on its eminent advantage of invisibility. The submarine is thus in a position to carry on the war against the enemy's communications in all sea areas, including areas of undisputed enemy domination.

292 - Free

293 - The enemy seeks to counter the danger of submarine operations on the routes of solitary ships, by arming the ships, in order to prevent the successful use of the submarine's gunnery, and to compel the submarine to use the more expensive torpedo, thus reducing its chances of success and its effective stay in the theatre of operations.

294 - Another defensive measure of the enemy against the use of the submarine in the war on merchant shipping is the formation of convoys under the protection of war-ships. As a result of the concentration of numerous steamers to form convoys, the sea routes lose their characteristic peacetime appearance and become desolate, as it is only at relatively long intervals that a concentration of steamers passes along them.

To achieve decisive successes against such concentrations of steamers, a concentration of submarines is necessary, because the lone submarine can only achieve partial success against a convoy.

295 - The general rule for the use and the offensive operations of the submarine in the war against merchant shipping is to station the submarines, whenever possible, at points where the traffic is thickest. In doing this, the submarines should be free

The conclusion to 16 sausages is a cigarette! "Here, are you coming for a drag?" With one stuck behind his ear, the navigator's mate asks his pal if he wants to go for a smoke in the tower, which is made available when they are on the surface. He is humorous fellow, always ready for a joke with coarse words and however grim he looks when at sea he is good-hearted chap.

and mobile in their operations, while in narrow coastal waters, on the other hand, their positions should be stationary.

296 - If a sufficient number of submarines is available, they must assemble on the enemy sea routes at a sufficient depth, but also in sufficient breadth, to be able to contact enemy sea traffic, which, in wartime, will avoid the usual peace routes, make long detours, and come from many different directions.

297 - Within range of our own air bases, where air reconnaissance of the enemy sea communications is practicable, extensive mutual support by the air arm and the submarines in the common war against enemy overseas trade will be possible.

Leisure time! In the U-room they are playing skat. Two "commentators" look on from the control room through the corridor. Their watch makes it possible, as one of the two petty officers is at the communal table waiting for the "smoking salon" in the tower to become available. The leather clothes for the off duty men hang on all port side protrusions in the narrow space. Left of the two control room petty officers' bunks, the green curtain hangs, pushed aside.

298 - Free

299 - Free

300 - Free

b) How to proceed when stopping Steamers

In waging war on enemy shipping, act according to the prize regulations, if sinking without warning is not allowed.

301 - In war, it is a fundamental rule that every steamer is suspect. When stopping steamers, the commander must therefore behave with due caution, in spite of his eagerness to use his boat for purpose of attack.

302 - Submarine traps must everywhere be expected, camouflaged in all possible ways. Steamers of all types and sizes can be adapted for this purpose. The experiences in this field can never be regarded as final. Attention is called to the booklet 'War Experiences 1914-18.'

303 - Every steamer which is intended to be stopped must first be inspected underwater at dose quarters, for the purpose of determining the type, nationality (method of fixing the neutrality marks, name, etc., for example, whether absolutely fixed, or interchangeable), and armament, with an eye to suspicious superstructures, suspicious (cabin) windows, etc. In doing this, at least two torpedoes should be ready for immediate launching.

304 - When the first careful inspection of the steamer under water has been carried out, the submarine surfaces at a sufficient distance astern of the steamer - of under 4,000m - and stops it.

305 - In order to ensure against surprise moves, attention should be paid to the following:

a. Act quickly and resolutely, losing no time. Any attempted resistance is to be ruthlessly smashed. The steamer is already offering resistance, and must be treated as an enemy: if it does not stop immediately; if it makes use of wireless telegraphy, even if, in that case, only its name and position are given, without an actual submarine alarm; if it fails to obey instructions as to course; or if the steamer's boat, on being summoned, is not launched with the necessary promptitude. Do not, therefore, wait too long before firing the first live shot, but, if the circumstances require it, be quick to lend emphasis to the instructions issued, through the medium of the guns.

b. Do not go on board a steamer for the purpose of carrying out investigations, not even if the ship appears to be abandoned. Always ask for the papers to be seen in one of the ship's boats.

c. During the whole time that a steamer is being stopped, keep at a distance - not under 4,000m - and always show the steamer the narrow outline of the submarine. Always keep the submarine's engines going; do not manoeuvre over the stern.

d. The submarine should always try to keep in line with the masts of the steamer, to prevent artillery opposition (only the stern gun of the steamer can be used). Every movement of the steamer - apparent broaching to should be answered by a counter-manoeuvre (stationary ships naturally turn broadside on to the sea). If such movements are repeated in a suspicious way, open fire at once with live ammunition.

e. Always be ready for an emergency dive.

f. No superfluous hands on deck.

g. Keep the sharpest possible lookout in all directions: horizon, sky and sea, including the immediate neighbourhood (possibility of cooperation of the steamer with submarine traps, patrol ships of all kinds, submarines and airplanes). The lookout must not allow itself to be diverted for one moment from its exclusive task of keeping watch, by the happenings during the stopping of the steamer.

h. In bad visibility, special caution and alertness is necessary. The gunnery fire may be heard by ships which happen to be in the neighbourhood, but not in sight, and these ships may suddenly arrive at top speed.

i. A specially reliable man should be assigned the exclusive task of watching the steamer after it has been stopped.

j. A close watch should be kept on the crew of the boat coming alongside, in order to be able effectively to counter any hostile action, such as the throwing of hand grenades, explosives, etc. (Automatic pistols and tommy guns should always ready at hand on the conning tower.)

306 - The most important provisions of the prize regulations must have been thoroughly studied and memorized by the commander. Do not begin to consult books on the conning tower after stopping a steamer, that costs valuable time.

307 - Regarding the use of the submarine's guns, refer to section V, Nos. 271 to 279.

308 - If it had been decided to sink the steamer, it should be done quickly and efficiently, as a general rule, by torpedo at

The commander spends most of his time in his "room", the small niche beside the control room in the corridor towards the bow of the boat opposite the radio booth. It is as long as a person needs for sleeping in. There are no closed spaces on the U-Boat. In his bunk he relaxes or sits at his folding writing table and reads. The lockers are fitted in the back rest and along the upper curve of the pressure cabin to accommodate all that he needs. He has already pulled on his waterproof trousers, and jacket and sou'wester hang beside him. He is ready to grab them and rush up to the bridge if something occurs.

point-blank range ("Fangschuss"). For this purpose, approach the steamer underwater to within close range. The immediate vicinity of the steamer is the danger zone, to Which the submarine traps pin their hopes.

309 - If, in exceptional circumstances, it becomes necessary to sink a steamer with high explosive cartridges, the following points should be borne in mind:

a. For big ships, do not use only one cartridge, as the effect is too small.

b. Arrange the H.E. cartridges in bundles (three cartridges tied together are sufficient), and drop them, if the ship has a list, to a depth of at least 1m at the side of the ship which is out of the water. In order to produce the maximum explosive effect, the cartridges must always be firmly fixed to the objective. Damage to the ship's side above water is usually only slight, and ineffective.

c. Do not place H.E. cartridges in cabins or rooms, because in this case their detonation produces no effect worth speaking of. Below, simply open the sea-cocks, if there is time.

d. In using cartridge bundles, always use and detonate only one fuse. If a second fuse is detonated simultaneously with the first, the effect of the detonations, which take place in juxtaposition and, in part, cancel each other out, is considerably reduced.

e. Place bundles of cartridges near the largest spaces in the ship, i.e., the hold and the engine room. Take care that the air can get out of the rooms when the water rushes in after the explosion by breaking the glass of the port hole.

c) How to deal with Convoys

310 - The most important task within which the submarine is faced on sighting enemy convoys is to attack them, and to endeavour to repeat the attack again and again. The submarine must not allow itself to be shaken off. If it is temporarily repulsed or forced to submerge, it must continue to press on, again and again, in the direction of the general course of the convoy, seek to contact it, and renew the attack.

311 - In keeping contact with convoys, and carrying out the attacks, no attention should be paid to consumption of fuel, provided that enough fuel is saved to enable the submarine to return to its base.

312 -

a. On sighting convoys and other important objectives, in order that these may be attacked by other submarines as well, the submarine should report the sighting immediately, even before attacking itself, and send further reports confirming the contact, in the intervals between its attacks on the enemy ships.

b. Failing orders to the contrary, the most important thing always is to attack. Each submarine should be concerned primarily with carrying out its own attack. Exceptions, for example, for boats whose task it is to maintain the contact with the convoy, must be in accordance with orders from Headquarters.

c. For the information of other boats, the intention to attack should be communicated by short signals according to the 'Short Signal Book,' pages 1,4 and 83. The possible disadvantage of warning the enemy by these wireless messages is bound to be less serious than when, as a result of the omission of the messages, other submarines fail to contact the targets at all.

313 - The success, or otherwise, of the attacks of all the other submarines operating against the convoy depends on the skill of the first submarine, whose duty it is to keep the contact with the convoy.

314 -

    a. The essential contents of the reports must always

The skat board lies on the edge of the bunks in front of the horizontal sleepers perhaps, with two petty officers and a seaman from the bow at the partly unfolded table. The lamp rocks peacefully with the light sway of the boat; the loudspeaker under the ceiling transmits the shortwave radio programme from home until midnight or if the reception is poor, record music. Everyone who wants to go from the galley to the engines or vice-versa has to thread himself through the seated men. The metal ladders in front of the bunks, are to prevent the sleeping men from falling out. However, one or the other of them sometimes rolls over into the opposite bunk and then into the one beneath.

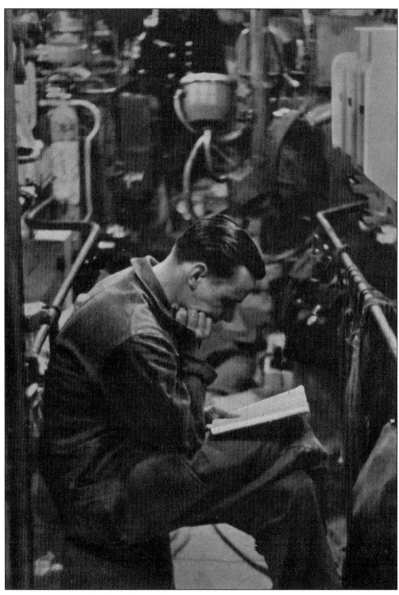

The engine watch, e.g., those in the e-engine room, do not usually have much to do apart from just watch, i.e., be prepared. If the engine telegraph rings or even the alarm, then they have to leap up and pull their levers. The engine watch is every six hours. Uncountable numbers of novels pass from hand to hand. The coffee sack in the corridor makes a terrific seat. But in a storm, the dripping wet waterproofs of the bridge watch hang right and left over the protective bars, because the e-room is the warmest in the whole boat.

be: Position, course, and speed on the enemy. Type, strength, and distribution of the enemy covering forces, and the state of the weather should be reported later to supplement these messages. Attention should be paid to the conditions of visibility and the resulting possibilities of error in estimating the distance for the reports on the position of the enemy.

b. Try to ascertain the general course of the enemy as soon as possible, from the reckoning, and report it as such (see Section II, B, No. 115).

315 - While carrying out its own attack, the submarine must transmit regular and complete contact reports, according to the following headings:

a. The two first boats to make contact, acting as "contact holders," transmit complete hourly reports.

b. As long as the two first boats transmit contact reports, the other boats signal "made contact!" once only, as soon as they have reached the convoy, or, analogously, "lost contact!", using short signals in both cases.

c. If a "contact holder" fails to send reports for longer than 1 hour, another boat must take over. This must be done without waiting for orders.

d. If a "contact holder" loses contact, it must report as soon as possible the last position of the enemy, and his course and speed.

e. All boats which have been in contact with the convoy, and lost ground in consequence of their long stay underwater, or have been driven off, must also report their own position.

316 - The "contact holders" also operate as is best for the purposes of their attack. Do not endanger your own overhauling

manoeuvre, and the success of the attack, by approaching too close, in order to obtain (more) accurate firing data.

317 - The arrangements for guiding further submarines to the spot are greatly facilitated by the emission of off signals by the submarine maintaining the contact. At intervals of half an hour, the "contact holder" sends out off signals and a wireless signal, on a long wave-length fixed by Headquarters, defining the off and the distance from the enemy, according to 'Standing War Orders for Submarine Commanders' ("St.Kriegsbor.B.d.U."), either at the request of other submarines, or on orders of the "Horne Submarine Command," or, in certain circumstances, on its own initiative if such orders are not received in time, and there is reason to believe that there are other submarines about. If the commander decides to send out off signals on his own initiative, the other submarines should first be notified by means of a wireless message or signal on the submarine's short wave.

318 - The transmission of off signals, however, always creates an additional danger that the "contact holder" will be spotted; consequently:
   a. Do not ask for off signals if dead reckoning and visibility are good.
   b. Ask for D/F signals if the dead reckoning is wrong, visibility is very bad, or if nothing is sighted on the computed point of contact ("erkoppelter Treffpunkt").

319 - The following are the rules for keeping the contact, and overhauling:
   a. Overhaul right on the limits of the zone of visibility. Be absolutely sure that you are not sighted.
   b. Keep the contact by the mast-tops or the smoke from the

funnels. The smoke is quite sufficient. If it disappears temporarily, it does not mean that you have lost contact. Go forward only after nothing has been seen for a certain length of time, and regain contact.

c. Keep the sharpest possible lookout, so as to see the masts, and to be able to tell when they increase in

The e-engineer not only loves to discuss technical details with his men but also to tell stories from back home now and again. Here, it is warm and comfortable and not as loud as in the diesel room next door so that it is easy to be heard. The hammock sways heavily over their heads, filled with biscuits and crisp-bread. The backrests are the levers, if one sits on the bar in front of them. The others squat on sacks and crates on the floor, because every single bit of free space is used for provisions when the boat goes out to sea. There are no special seats or stools.

height, and then to make off at full speed. At the same time, endeavour to lose no ground, but to get to the fore. If the distance from the enemy continues to be insufficient, submerge - go down to periscope depth. As soon as the position is clear, surface again.

d. If your position is behind the convoy, do not allow yourself to be driven too far back by the rear covering forces, but submerge in good time. In this way, you avoid, to a great extent, loss of ground, and gain time for a continuance of the pursuit.

e. Keep the sharpest possible lookout in the direction away from the enemy. In this direction, surprises may easily occur as a result of the enemy's sending out escorting vessels to a considerable distance, on the flanks and astern of the convoy, or as a result of the arrival of long-distance escorting units. Behaviour of the submarine is according to c).

320 - Apart from the clever tactics on the part of the submarine engaged in maintaining the contact with, and overhauling, the convoy, a decisive factor in the use of other submarines is faultless navigation on the part of both the "contact holder" and all the other boats. In the theatre of operations, it is therefore the imperative duty of the commander to seize on all possibilities for the purpose of ensuring efficient navigation. This necessitates, whenever possible, repeated reckonings during the day. A feeling for loss of speed and drift owing to the motion of the sea should be cultivated.

If errors of reckoning are discovered, the contact reports should be rectified at once, and attention called to the previous error; this should also be done, in case of necessity, by other submarines which detect false reckonings in the reports of the "contact holder" proper.

The chief engineer and his petty officers look for the damage which was discovered. For this reason the boat has surfaced. Soon they will take half the diesel apart and hammer and bang and file. "The forge in the Atlantic" the sailor calls it, and uses the time for sleep.

321 - For the rules of action governing the procedure of attack, see instructions in Section I, B, Nos. 25 and 35, Section II, B: "Use of the Submarine for the Underwater Attack," Nos. 105 to 124, as well as Section II, C, Nos. 134 to 136.

322 - The object of every overhauling manoeuvre is to attack as soon as possible; this important object should not be jeopardized by carelessness. Consequently, it is better to stay further out in the overhauling manoeuvre than to go too dose in, and run the risk of being spotted and forced to submerge, thus losing leeway for the attack, and time.

323 - It is only in case of inescapable necessity that the attack should be put off, for example, at dusk - if it is already too dark for the underwater launching of torpedoes - with the object of carrying out a surface attack with more certainty of success after darkness has fallen; or at dawn - if it is already too light for a sure aim at close quarters on the surface - with the object of carrying out a safe underwater attack at short range as soon as it gets light enough for that purpose (see Section II, B, No. 105, d).

324 - If the enemy's air and sea escort is so strong that it is not possible to overhaul in daytime, the attack should be postponed until nightfall. Nevertheless, for this purpose, the submarine should overhaul in good time during the day. At the least, it should be level with the convoy when twilight comes. The overhauling manoeuvre should not be put off till evening. There is a danger of being compelled to submerge, or of having to retreat to a distance, in consequence of the enemy's reconnaissance patrols, thus losing contact with the convoy.

325 - If the submarine is temporarily compelled to submerge

by the escorting forces of the enemy, it should not remain down too long. Surface again as soon as the position allows, in order to advance more quickly, and take up a position for the attack,' and also in order to observe better, and to be able to transmit contact reports.

326 - It is possible to keep the contact with the convoy in spite of the enemy's covering forces, or his air escort. The conditions for attack are, indeed, rendered more difficult by the presence of a strong escort, and by air cover, and more time is needed to mount the attack, but it is still possible, if the submarine commander acts with steadfastness and determination, to keep the contact. If the attack can no longer be successfully carried out by day, the submarine must get in a torpedo at night.

a. In the neighbourhood of the convoy, no submarine must be deterred from carrying out an attack by the fact that the enemy ASDIC operations have been observed. The distance of an adversary engaged in ASDIC hunting cannot be ascertained; the wireless D/F computer receives the enemy D/F at a greater distance than the latter can cover in target finding. For example, the enemy, while carrying out his D/F operations, may occupy a position well beyond the dip of the horizon, and have not located the submarine at all. Always remember, therefore, that the enemy can only attack what he sees, and that the submarine is more difficult to make out than he is himself. Consequently, the submarine commander should rely on himself and his lookout, and not become the slave of an instrument.

327 - If, for any reason, the submarine has failed to contact the enemy during the night, that is not a reason for giving up the attack. The submarine should keep obstinately on the track

Each of the men, not only the petty officers (engine room) and chief engineer, are specialists in their field, often trained mechanics, engineers etc.; now they are going to sea against the enemy. As an amateur, it is impossible to believe what these labourers, sailors and soldiers achieve by themselves far out in the Atlantic; they carry out the most complicated repairs that become necessary, under extremely difficult conditions.

of the enemy. The chase may go on for days before the first success is achieved against a convoy.

328 - In keeping the contact, the greatest care should be exercised during the transition from day to night, especially in the Atlantic, in southern latitudes. Here the twilight is so short that the transition from day to night comes with the utmost suddenness. At nightfall, the submarine maintaining the contact is therefore still at a distance almost equal to the appropriate distance by day and must go close in at once, resolutely and at top speed.

The possibility must always be reckoned with that the enemy will go well out and double after dark, effecting, apart from the zigzag movements as far observed, an important change of course, in order to shake off any pursuing submarines. In addition, at sunset (and perhaps during the day, if visibility becomes poor), the enemy will usually send out fast vessels of the escort, which search the sea in the rear of the convoy with the object of forcing any pursuing submarines underwater until the convoy is out of sight, and has carried out, unnoticed, the usual evening change of course. These escort vessels sent out to reconnoiter, and shake off submarine "contact holders," always return to the convoy, feigning to take a different course.

329 - When engaged in operations against convoys, based on contact reports, the meeting point with the convoy should always be fixed sufficiently far ahead of it, according to the conditions of visibility, for example 10 to 14sm.

330 - If a submarine, on receipt of contact reports, is a good distance ahead of the convoy, it must exercise care in going to meet it, as otherwise it may easily lose ground by advancing too far.

331 - Troublesome sweepers of the enemy escort must be destroyed, if an opportunity offers to attack them. The destruction of covering ships, above all, of cruiser escorts, destroyers, etc., is in the interests of all the submarines which are already in contact with the convoy, or are to be used to attack it.

332 -

a. Submarine traps must also be reckoned with in dealing with convoys. These have instructions to station themselves among the last steamers, and to fall behind, pretending that they have engine trouble, etc., in order thus to attract attacking submarines, to lead them away from the convoy, and to be able to attack them. Be cautious, therefore, when attacking steamers sailing behind convoys.

b. It has been observed that groups of escort ships, emitting clouds of smoke, frequently collect behind convoys for the purpose of deceiving the submarines, and drawing them away from the convoy. The commander must not be led astray by these tactics. In case he is not certain that he is in contact with the convoy, he should make up his contact report accordingly: for example, "big clouds of smoke" or "ships belching smoke."

333 - If several boats are being used in the attack, none of them must break off the pursuit merely because it has used up its torpedoes. It must follow the convoy, seeking to contact it, and maintain the contact. As there is no longer a target, it should take up the most favourable position as a "contact holder" (for example, sun, convoy and submarine in time), and continue to send messages. The boat will be ordered back as soon as possible.

The engine is ready again and can show what it can do! The watch that repaired it, is proud of their achievement and rightly so. For hours they worked very hard, sweating and oil-smeared. There was "Kujambel", juice. But now the engine will be photographed with the chief engineer who worked just as hard as they did. Only then will it be cleaned, and before going to bed – the next watch is coming up – something good will be "sanded down", in the empty, nocturnal bunks next door. They have earned it! No alcohol is given out on board during a mission against the enemy.

334 - When contact has been lost, a systematic search must be made by the submarines. The commander must first form a clear idea of the position, on the basis of his own observations and the reports of the other boats. After that, the submarine should carry out reconnaissance patrols at top speed. In poor visibility, and at night, submerge frequently, and listen (sound-location). Do not give up if D/F sound location at first fails to produce results. Submerge again, and follow up.

335 - If other boats are encountered during the pursuit of a convoy, go within signalling range or earshot. Compare notes. Arrange reconnaissance.

Quickly, before they dive, the petty officer washes the worst of the grime from his body. Once they are on the surface, bowls and water will not stand still so willingly! During a trip, there is normally only 3 litres of warm, freshwater available every three weeks for each man to wash in; if he wants to. Washing teeth and body with salt water or with the fresh water from the torpedoes that has oil in it, is no pleasure but has to do for the rest of the time.

336 - Conjectures and positive indications as to the position of the convoy (for example, sightings of aircraft, track of steamers, solitary ships, results of sound location, detonations, star shells), and the courses of unsuccessful reconnaissance patrols, should be reported by W.T. Report all particulars likely to be of use in clarifying the position, more especially when it emerges from an order to attack that the impression of the position at headquarters is erroneous. A clear conception of the tactical possibilities of the situation is a pre-condition for the transmission of correct reports.

337 - As soon as the impression is created that contact can only be made by means of a guided attack, and not by submarines acting on their own initiative, orders are issued prescribing certain groupings (see No. 349 and following according to "Instructions for Naval Warfare" ("S.A." II C), there is the method of directional reconnaissance, and reconnaissance in sectors.

338 - In the directional reconnaissance method, each submarine is allotted a certain strip of the area to be searched, in which it must carry out a systematic search at high speed, on a zigzag course, for an enemy presumed to pass through a certain limited zone. The number and angle of the zigzags, and consequently the thoroughness of the search, depends on weather and visibility, and the speed margin of the submarine.

339 - When the area to be searched is divided, for the above purpose, into sectors, one sector is dealt with by each submarine, the apex of the sector being the last known position of the convoy. If at all possible, the search should be commenced at the apex of the sector. The sector should be covered by the submarine in both zigzags and in "strips," until the whole area

During the time submerged, the W.O. In the control room "goes" on his watch in the control room. There is nothing particular happening, otherwise the C.E. would sit here instead, and instead of the one helmsmen, there would be two, operating the stern and bow rudders. At the moment they have submerged for a few hours until the weather improves, because the visibility is too bad. The officer reads. He sits, as does the helmsman, on a green leather cushion above the map cupboard. Everything is peaceful and quiet. Barely a sound can be heard apart from the humming of the transformer. Whoever is off duty, uses the time and the boat's wonderfully, static position, to grab some sleep.

has been searched up to the highest limits of the reported course of the enemy, then it should carry the search to the boundaries of the sector for the high rates of speed. As soon as the upper limit is reached, remain there until the convoy must be assumed to have passed through the sector at low rates of speed; or begin the inward search.

a. The submarines may only abandon an operation which they have been ordered to carry out when the necessity to do so is inescapable. In such cases the abandonment of the operation must be reported immediately. If a submarine is of the opinion that it is inadvisable to continue an operation assigned to it by the command, for special reasons that are unknown to the latter, it must mention the reasons and ask for fresh orders.

b. The replacement of torpedoes while the submarine is keeping the contact must not result in the loss of the contact; consequently:

   I. If at all possible, reloading should be effected above water, while maintaining the contact. At the same time, care should be taken that the submarine is always ready to submerge.

   II. If the state of the weather compels the submarine to dive for the purpose of reloading, then only as many torpedoes should be loaded at once as will not interrupt the contact with the convoy. For example: first submerge, then reload a torpedo, then surface, then follow the convoy, and then, after catching up with it, load again.

   III. If an improvement in the weather is in sight, wait to recharge until this is possible on the surface, in case there is then still a chance to attack.

   IV. All preparations for reloading torpedoes are to be made before submerging!

SECTION VIII
OPERATING IN PACKS; RECONNAISSANCE AND ATTACK

a) General

340 - The object of the common attack is to produce contact between a number of submarines and an adversary who has been located by a submarine or another reconnaissance unit, to maintain that contact, and to destroy the enemy.

This object is attained by holding on obstinately to the enemy, and by the transmission of unambiguous messages by the "contact holder," as well as by immediate action of the other submarines, on their own initiative, after receipt of the first contact report. A special order calling for such independent action is only required in exceptional circumstances.

The pre-condition of success is - in addition to an aggressive spirit, a capacity for making quick decisions, initiative, tenacious endurance, and unfailing skill - the will to summon the other boats to the attack, in addition to carrying out your own attack.

341 - In carrying out common operations against the enemy, there is no distinction between reconnaissance and attack. If, in certain circumstances, only one of these tasks can be carried out, the attack has unconditional priority.

Departures from this fundamental rule must be specially authorized in each individual case.

b) System of Command

342 - The distribution and grouping of the submarine, and the

operational and tactical command, is ordinarily in the hands of the submarine Command ("B.d.U.").

Groups
343 - If there is a considerable number of submarines, a subdivision in "submarine groups" may be made.

Group Commanders
344 - When group commanders are appointed for this purpose by the Submarine Command, they assume the tactical direction of their groups. If no group commanders are appointed, the tactical command of the individual groups remains in the hands of the Submarine Command.

If a group commander is prevented from giving orders, and does not appear on the scene, his duties are taken over by the Submarine Command, unless a substitute has been specially appointed.

A few pages of the novel from the boat's library before going to sleep. That doesn't stop Paul from participating in the general joking going on in the U-room. He is a reservist, a professional sailor: a reason to constantly rib the "young activists". He stands above them all with his dry, barbed, warmhearted humour.

345 - The tactical command of the group commanders should be limited to taking steps to relocate the enemy, when contact has been lost; for example, by organizing reconnaissance or advance patrols.

The group commanders must send in a report to the Submarine Command, when the situation is such that it cannot be taken in by the command on land.

346 - An order issued by the Submarine Command overrides an order by a group commander.

The control room petty officer on his watch, leans smiling, day in day out, in his typical position over the map desk of his kingdom, that is filled with complicated equipment. He has a joking remark for everyone in every situation. He saves the atmosphere when it starts to go flat. With 14 missions under his belt, he has been wearing the Iron Cross for a long time! An irrepressible joker and an equally reliable, knowledgeable man filled with a sense of responsibility. A priceless amalgam! If there is something happening, then he hardly allows himself time to sleep, even during his off-duty time.

347 - Free

348 - Free

c) Taking Up Action Stations: Method and Formation

Formation

349 - There is no hard and fast rule for the common attack. To facilitate the direction of the operations, however, the following - area of attack, action stations, waiting stations, reconnaissance patrol(s), advance patrol(s) - in certain areas with "centre of gravity".

350 - In all attack formations the positions are occupied singly (one boat at a time).

Area of attack

351 - The area of attack is that part of the theatre of operations of the submarines which is assigned to one submarine.

This method is adopted when large sea areas are to be patrolled and no precise data are available regarding the enemy traffic.

The area of attack of the individual submarine is defined in squares, latitude and longitude, or by other limits. If the areas of attack are defined as squares of a certain "depth," the term "depth" means the diameter of the area with the prescribed square as its centre. Example: "Area of attack square X depth 20sm" means: The area of attack is bounded by a circle with a radius of 10sm about the centre of the square X.

Freedom of movement, and Authority to attack in the area of attack

352 - Within its allotted area each submarine has full freedom

of movement, in order to seek its own targets. Every worthwhile target must be attacked.

Evacuation of the area of attack

353 - The submarine must leave the area of attack:

    a. for the purpose of attacking an enemy, and of prosecuting the attack (pursuing the enemy), if the submarine is itself in contact, or has been in contact, with the enemy.

    b. for the purpose of carrying out independent operations against *convoys and concentrations of warships*, concerning which reports have been received from other submarines, or from the Submarine Command ("B.d.U."), if those convoys or warships are within reach.

On the completion of the attacks, the submarine must go back into the reconnaissance area.

354 - A submarine may leave its area of attack when special circumstances, or particularly efficient counteraction of the enemy, make it impossible for it to stay there. The evacuation of the area of attack must then be reported as soon as possible.

355 - Free

Distribution of Action Stations

356 - The object of the "distribution of action stations" is to contact a particular enemy unit, *which must be mentioned in the instructions (order)*.

Action stations are defined in the instructions (order) in squares of a certain depth (see No. 351) or other geographical points with a certain depth.

Taking up action stations

357 - If the instructions issued by the Command do not provide for a special formation of the submarines, and for special positions, the positions are occupied in the order of the boat numbers, i.e., the submarine with the lowest number occupies the position first indicated, the submarine with the next lowest number the second position, and so on.

If the instructions specify a certain time of day, the positions should be taken up by that time.

Operating from action stations

358 - The submarine must operate from the action station, against the target indicated in the instructions, as soon as the target is reported.

Whatever position you lie in, with the warm, soft fur jacket behind your neck, wrapped in the eternally-damp, woollen blanket, a drop of water from the boat occasionally falls onto your face. Jack Seaman goes to sleep immediately in any position, however wonderful the sea is, amidst the loudest noise from his comrades and the radiogram, in order to recuperate his strength.

Authority to attack from action stations

359 - Targets other than those mentioned in the instructions (order) should be attacked:

    a. When the attack on the main target is not thereby endangered;

    b. When a target is found which is approximately as valuable as the prescribed target.

    c. When the targets are warships from cruisers upwards.

Abandoning action stations

360 - The action stations may be abandoned for the purpose of prosecuting the attack on these targets, if they have been sighted by the submarine itself, as wen as in the cases defined in No. 354.

361 - Limitations or extensions of the authority to attack are provided for in the operational order.

Ready to land once more. The bo'sun and chief engineer are already looking out for a mooring. By God and Saint Anna, the music band has formed up to greet us!

362 - Free

363 - Free

Waiting Station

364 - The "waiting station" is a preliminary position before taking up action stations. It is used when precise details of a given target are not available, and when the Submarine Command wishes to reserve its decision as regards the attack, after receiving reports about important targets.

The distributions and the taking up of "waiting stations" are subject to the same rules as apply to taking up action stations (see Nos. 356, 357).

Authority to attack from waiting station

365 - Failing special orders, the boats are authorized to attack, from their waiting stations, any target approximately as valuable as the target of the submarines on action stations, warships from cruisers upwards, and other targets, if the attack on the latter does not interfere with the subsequent attack on the target prescribed for the submarines on "waiting station."

Abandoning the waiting station

366 - A submarine may only abandon its waiting station:

    a. In the prosecution of an attack on one of the targets specified in No. 359, provided the submarine has itself made contact.

    b. On orders of the Submarine Command, or of a group commander who is authorized accordingly:

    c. In the cases mentioned in No. 354.

367 - Free

368 - Free

Centre of gravity

369 - If a "centre of gravity" is provided for in the order, the submarine must operate, in the first place, round the "centre of gravity." If they there encounter a strong defence, or see no chance of a successful attack, they may temporarily carry out raids in every direction within the boundaries of their areas, but they should always return afterwards to the "centre of gravity."

Reconnaissance and Vanguard patrols ("A.St." or "Vp.St.")

370 - Reconnaissance and vanguard patrols are carried out for the purpose of patrolling large sea areas, with sound-location, as well as of contacting certain targets.

In the instructions (order) their patrols are identified by starting points and terminal points. The boat first mentioned in the order occupies the starting point, the boat last mentioned the terminal point. The other boats take up equidistant stations, in the sequence indicated in the order, between the starting point and the terminal point.

Advance and Direction of Advance of Reconnaissance Patrol

371 - The direction and speed of advance of a reconnaissance patrol are given in the order as "course" and "speed." They should be adhered to as an average course and an average speed of the individual submarine in crossing the area.

If the order calls for an advance by position lines, the position lines must be reached at the prescribed times, after which the average course and speed of the individual submarine should be calculated with regard to the current, the motion of the sea, and the wind.

Vanguard patrols, in contradistinction to the reconnaissance patrols, do not change their stations

Radius of Action of Reconnaissance Patrols and Advance Patrols

372 - The reconnaissance area of the individual submarine on reconnaissance patrol and advance patrol, comprises the distance from the point computed for the individual boat, towards both sides in the direction of the patrol, to a point situated halfway between the submarine and the next submarine; for the first and last boat, the reconnaissance area extends, by half the distance of the space between the boats, beyond the starting and terminal points.

Vertically to the reconnaissance and advance patrols, there is in general no such thing as operational "depth," except insofar as it is necessary to enable the individual submarine to accomplish its tasks according to No. 373.

"Depth" in the area of the reconnaissance and advance patrols

If, by way of exception, a "depth" is provided for in the instructions for the reconnaissance and advance patrols the size of the reconnaissance area (reconnaissance range) of the individual submarine is adjusted according to No. 351.

Operational instructions for the individual submarine on reconnaissance and advance patrol

373 - Regularized movements of the individual submarine in its reconnaissance area are not necessary unless expressly called for in the instructions, by way of exception. It is only necessary, in the reconnaissance area, to maintain the average course and speed.

For the rest, each submarine must operate in a manner best suited to the conditions obtaining in its reconnaissance area. This purpose can be served by: travelling to and from in the direction of the advance patrol, zigzagging in the forward direction in the reconnaissance area, carrying out sorties toward the dark horizon, submerging for sound-location, judicious choice of courses in regard to the wind and the motion of the sea. At the same time, the engines should be used with the utmost economy. The use of higher speeds must be specially called for in the instructions.

Authority to attack, and evacuation of positions in the reconnaissance and advance patrols.

374 - Every worthwhile target must be attacked, unless there are special instructions limiting the objectives.

Each submarine must evacuate its reconnaissance area:

    a. for the purpose of attacking an enemy with whom it is itself in contact, or has been;

    b. for the purpose of attacking convoys and concentrations of warships reported inside the reconnaissance area or advance patrol area.

On the completion of the attacks, the submarine must return to the reconnaissance area.

d) How to act in the Area of Operation before and during Contact with the Enemy

Remain invisible

375 - It is a fundamental rule to remain unseen, in every position, until the submarine carries out its attack. Consequently, the action of the individual submarine is governed by the rules laid down in Section I, B.

Freedom of movement

376 - Within the limits of their own areas, the submarines act on their own initiative. They should seek the most favourable conditions for attack, in accordance with the rules for the

various positions, on the basis of their estimation of the position of the enemy, the defence, the state of the weather, and other circumstances. There is plenty of scope here for the penetration and skill of the commander.

A six-weeks beard – the commander wears one, as do all his men!

The first cigarette in the open air tastes good for the diesel room petty officer wearing his life jacket for the area that is mined. He has not stood outside since they went out. However, all the difficulties are soon forgotten; the trip was not in vain. That knowledge brings pride and happiness.

160

Authority to attack

377 - The authority to attack contained in the rules for taking up the different positions, means, at the same time, an order to attack.

In cases of genuine doubt, the commander must decide in favour of attacking. A successful attack is always a gain -a neglected opportunity cannot be made good.

General reports

378 - In making reports, the commander must always ask himself the following questions:

a. To what extent is the command, and to what extent are the other submarines, informed of the position?

b. What do the command and the other submarines require to know about a new position?

c. Will the transmission of my message now and here be bad for any of the other boats? Is my message so important that I must accept that?

d. What else is there of importance to the command if I decide to send a message? For example, weather, shipping (naval) successes, fuel position, available torpedoes.

e. After formulating and before transmitting the message: have I expressed myself as briefly, and, above all, as clearly as possible, or may I be misunderstood?

379 - For the command, it is important to know exactly at clues the enemy may have to the positions of submarines.

Submarines which have undoubtedly been sighted by the enemy in the area of operations, must therefore report this by short signal.

380 - Free

Keeping the contact with important objectives

382 - Without prejudice to the attack which the submarine has been detailed to carry out, which always has priority, the submarine must make contact with important objectives.

Important objectives are:

    a. Convoys.

    b. Concentrations of Warships.

    c. The targets mentioned in the order to take up stations.

If contact is also to be maintained with other targets, and other submarines are to attack outside their own areas, instructions to this effect will be issued in the operation order, or in a special order.

If a submarine makes contact with an important enemy, all submarines within striking distance begin to cooperate - the great hour of the submarine commanders and crews.

"Contact Holders"

383 - Without prejudice to its own attack, the "contact holding" submarine must use every means of maintaining contact with the target, following it, regaining contact if lost. It is on the skill and resolution of the "contact holder" that success depends more than on anything else.

Transmission of messages by "contact holders": see Nos. 314 and 315.

Maintaining contact in special cases

384 - The above instructions (order) requiring the submarine to keep the contact with important objectives do not exclude a decision on the part of the commander, to take advantage of special circumstances in individual cases (for example, damaged warships, big steamers (liners) for the purpose of maintaining

the contact and attacking at the same time. In such cases the command will issue orders saying whether the submarine is to continue to hold contact, or other boats are to operate against the reported objective.

Submitting reports without maintaining contact

385 - The operation order will state in which cases reports are to be submitted without maintaining contact.

Attack by the other boats

386 - On receipt of the first report of contact with an important objective, all submarines within range begin to operate against that objective. An order to attack is not needed. All limits of the operation areas, with the exception of the "waiting stations," are abolished. Only the submarines on "waiting station" must wait for the order to attack.

The commanders must not allow themselves to be deterred from attacking because of initial considerations of distance. It is known that submarines stationed at a distance of more than 400sm have carried out successful attacks against the objective.

In these attacks, all the skill and resolution of the commanders and crews, and their readiness to go into action, must be called into requisition, and lead to an annihilating success.

387 - Free
388 - Free
389 - Free
390 - Free

SECTION IX

USE (EXPENDITURE)
OF TORPEDOES

391 - Every possibility of attack must be used quickly and resolutely. In most theatres of operation, the opportunities of hitting with a torpedo are rare. Do not, therefore, economize in torpedoes when attacking.

392 - The torpedo must always be ready for action at shortest notice. Always be prepared for unexpected opportunities of attack. A neglected opportunity will not recur.

In foggy weather and bad visibility, the tubes should be ready flooded. If necessary, they should be flooded via the mouth flaps.

393 - As far as the supply of torpedoes allows, several discharges, in the form of multiple shots (double or three-fold shots) should be directed against worthwhile targets, even at short range and when the aiming data are not in doubt. In this case, all the torpedoes should hit the mark, in order to ensure the annihilation of the enemy. This means that the torpedoes should be fired at different parts of the target.

394 - If the range is over 1,000m, or if there is uncertainty as regards the aiming data (high speed of the enemy), several torpedoes (2, 3 or 4) should be released on the "fan" pattern. The idea is to make sure of one hit. It is better to score only one hit than to miss the target with each of several consecutive shots.

The target should therefore be covered by aiming at the boundaries of the area of dispersion on the target, i.e., the shots should be spread by the width of the dispersion area in relation to one shot aimed on the basis of the estimated data (if 2 or 4 shots are fired), in relation to an imaginary middle shot).

The early sunlight is glinting on the military band's instruments, the wharf is full of comrades, they stand crowded on the quayside - even the chief, the admiral himself, has come out to greet us! Boy oh boy, this is a real reception!

The courageous boat is moored, with its victory pennants flying on the raised periscope, one for each steamer sunk. The comrades have gone on land with their things, only the watch remains behind on the bridge. The boat will be repaired in the dock. Holidays beckon. But soon they will all want to get back out to sea!

395 - If a final shot is necessary to sink the damaged ship, remember that the number of misses at the kill is proportionately greater than in firing during the attack.

a. At the kill, steer the submarine ahead of the stationary target, in position 90 at range 2,000 to 3,000m, and approach slowly, carefully keeping the course, to find out whether the enemy is still making headway. When the change of bearing has been measured, the speed of the target should be set on the director angle of the computer, or the enemy should be finished off by the bow or stern torpedo attack proper. The speed of the enemy should be taken into account in determining the displacement of the marking point on the target.

b. Go in as close as possible, range under 1,000m. On moonlit nights and during the daytime, submerge once more and attack underwater at 400 to 500m.

c. If, in remote sea areas, an early arrival of enemy defence forces is not to be anticipated, the final shot should not be precipitated. Many ships sink only after 2 to 3 hours.

d. If enemy anti-submarine forces are sighted (naval or air), the final torpedo should be fired at once.

e. In the circumstances described under C, it should be ascertained whether the target can be destroyed by gunfire, instead of by the final torpedo. See also No. 277.

(Note: Amendments number 1, 2 and 4 were not included in the original transcribed copy.)

More from the same series

Most books from the 'Hitler's War Machine' series are edited and endorsed by Emmy Award winning film maker and military historian Bob Carruthers, producer of Discovery Channel's Line of Fire and Weapons of War and BBC's Both Sides of the Line. Long experience and strong editorial control gives the military history enthusiast the ability to buy with confidence.

Tiger I in Combat   Tiger I Crew Manual   Panzers at War 1939-1942   Panzers at War 1943-1945

Wolf Pack - the U boats   Poland 1939   Luftwaffe Combat Reports   Sturmgeschütze

German Artillery in Combat   Panzer Combat Reports   The Panther V in Combat   German Tank Hunters

The Afrika Korps in Combat   Panzers I & II   Panzer III   Panzer IV

For more information visit www.pen-and-sword.co.uk